STORAGE

STORAGE:

Great Ideas for Closets, Kitchens, Kids' Rooms, Bathrooms, and Every Room in the House

by Beth Franks

Chapter One by Stephanie Culp

HPBooks

A FRIEDMAN GROUP BOOK

Published by HPBooks
a division of
Price Stern Sloan, Inc.
360 North La Cienega Boulevard
Los Angeles, California 90048

Library of Congress Cataloging-in-Publication Data

Franks, Beth.
Storage : great ideas for closets, kitchens, kids' rooms, bathrooms, and
every room in the house.

Includes index.
1. Cabinet-work.   2. Shelving (for books).   3. Storage in the home.
4. Clothes closets.   I. Title.
TT197.F75   1988   684.1'6   87-24858
ISBN 0-89586-720-6
ISBN 0-89586-719-2 (pbk.)

*STORAGE: Great Ideas for Closests, Kitchens, Kids' Rooms, Bathrooms, and Every
Room in the House*
was prepared and produced by
Michael Friedman Publishing Group, Inc.
15 West 26th Street
New York, New York 10010

Editor: Tim Frew
Art Director: Mary Moriarty
Designer: Devorah Levinrad
Photo Editor: Christopher Bain
Production Manager: Karen L. Greenberg

Typeset by B.P.E. Graphics
Color separations by South Sea International Press Ltd.
Printed and bound in Hong Kong by Leefung-Asco Printers Ltd.

Dedication

In memory of Helen High, my grandmother, a long-time master of graceful and convenient storage.

Acknowledgements

Many people helped make this book a reality. I owe a lot to the many companies that offered helpful information and photographs. Nancy Kalish and Tim Frew at the Friedman Publishing Group were a source of support and encouragement. I'd also like to thank professional organizers Linda London and Maxine Ordesky, who provided valuable advice on customizing closets. The DIY projects were made possible thanks to the able assistance of my father, Jerry Franks, and brother-in-law, Jeff Young. And finally, special thanks to authors Deniece Schofield and Stephanie Culp, who initiated me into the world of organized living; their humorously practical approach was a constant inspiration in writing this book.

Darryl Baird

CONTENTS

CHAPTER 1
Storage: An Organized View

A place for everything, and everything in its place, is an age-old piece of wisdom that just about everyone has heard at least once in their lifetime. But, as with so many wise axioms that we hear and appreciate, it is often easier said than done. Obviously, storing everything in its proper place would be much simpler if we had adequate storage space to begin with.

However, sufficient storage space seems to magically diminish with each passing year, as we effortlessly accumulate belongings that we somehow feel are necessary to our daily lives. For those people who share the household with other family members, the accumulation is magnified by each family member —all contributing to the household reservoir of clothing, mementos, entertainment fixtures and gadgets, kitchen paraphernalia, papers, collections, hobby materials, and, of course, countless other "necessities."

Compounding the problem is an apparent lack of space to begin with. The average home today is not nearly as big as the grand old home of yesteryear, and apartment living has always left something to be desired when it comes to space of any kind. People living in large cities feel the full impact of too little space. While they tend to pare down their personal surplus out of sheer necessity, adequate storage space is still a dream for nearly all apartment dwellers.

Whatever the living circumstances, most people make do with an added shelf here or there, or an organizational gadget placed in what seems to be a strategic area of the home. Finally, in frustration, the day arrives when people convince themselves that there is "simply no more room" and they begin the search for a bigger and, inevitably, more expensive house or apartment.

Before joining the ranks of

Right: Closets often harbor wasted space. The ceiling to floor shelves in this pantry make optimum use of an existing area.

Brian Leatart

the relocated, reconsider the storage situation in your current residence. There is more than one way to view and ultimately attack the challenge of too little storage space. Given some time and thought, most people can at least triple the storage space in their current residence.

The logical first step to increasing storage space is to get organized. Go through and reassess the value of each of those "necessary" items. Do you use the item regularly? Does it have special meaning to you? Does it need fixing, and if it does, why haven't you fixed it? Does it fit, is it in style, and do you even like it? Does it require regular cleaning or maintenance that you no longer have time for? Does it enrich or add to your life, and for that matter, do you even use it? Could someone else get more pleasure and use from the item? Does it cost more in square footage to store it than it was ever worth in the first place?

The answers to these questions will undoubtedly free up a substantial measure of your current storage space. By getting rid of things that you have long ago outgrown or no longer have use for, you will rid yourself of useless items that no longer have a place in your life or in your available storage space. Have a garage sale, pick out a favorite charity and give them your castoffs, call your friends and relatives and tell them to take what they want, and jettison the leftover accumulation. The

Left: **This kitchen features restaurant-style storage that exploits every square inch of available space.**

Brian Leatart

Courtesy Quaker Maid

benefits will far outweigh the temporary pain of parting with your unnecessary stockpile of treasures—otherwise known as "stuff."

Just as the pioneers in covered wagons lightened their load to get to where they were going, you'll now be able to go forth on your quest for suitable storage space that will provide a home for your belongings as well as fit in with your décor.

Now that you have weeded out the excess in your life,

make an assessment of your current available storage space. Use a measuring tape to measure all of the interior cabinet storage areas. Designate specific areas for categories of items in each cabinet, and plan the space to accommodate all of the items that you own in that category. Don't forget to allow extra space for the future. You'll be adding to, more than you'll be taking from, your plethora of belongings. So whether it is stashed in the kitchen or the

Although they may not actually provide any more room, swing-out shelves installed in base cabinets will help organize kitchen storage for easy access.

Right: Many manufacturers offer specialty cabinets with their more expensive lines. Swing-out pantry shelves and pull-out trays are just two of the many options.

Courtesy J. Wood/WCI Cabinet Group

bedroom, work with the thought that there needs to be ''growing'' space in each storage facility.

While checking cabinet interiors, ask yourself if you are making the best use of the space that you now have. Shelf dividers, turntables, pull-out bins, and a host of other space-saving gadgets are available at minimal cost to enhance the organizational interior of your existing cabinetry. Adding a shelf in a too-deep cabinet area can also make a noticeable difference in space usage. For example, if the linen cabinet has two very deep shelves, chances are your towels and sheets tend to fall over in a distressing heap. An extra shelf or two in that cabinet will clear up the problem. Your sheets and towels can then be neatly organized, and the unsightly piles that used to greet you from within the linen cabinet will happily disappear. A simple shelf addition will not only clear up mess and clutter, it

will often provide just a bit more space because of the newly organized interior.

Next, cast your eye and measuring tape to the interiors of the closets. No one *ever* has enough closet space, and yet this is an area that can often be improved with dramatic results. Again, assuming that you have thinned out all of the things you no longer wear, divide your clothing into different categories. Slacks, shirts, blouses, skirts, and dresses should all be

Courtesy Techline/By Marshall Erdman and Associates, Inc.

Above: **Organize a clothes closet using a double rod system, with shelves for shoes and sweaters. Reserve the high shelf for little-used or seasonal items.**

Left: **Many custom closet systems offer mix-and-match components that adapt to individual needs and can be arranged to fit any space.**

grouped separately. Then consider installing double rods, with shirts on top, and pants below; shoe racks; sliding baskets; and any or all of the many closet space-saving devices and systems on the market today. Shelving in closets can hold sweaters, T-shirts, tennis togs, and much more. Cabinetry or shelving above the closet can often be improved upon by adding another shelf, or by making creative organizational use of plastic shoe boxes, lingerie

Courtesy Lillian Vernon Corp.

Left: You can hang twice as much in a closet with double rods. This model simply hooks over the existing upper rod and is segmented to keep clothes from crushing up against one another. *Below left:* Slatted shelves installed in the bottom of a closet keep shoes and handbags shipshape. *Below:* An ingenious solution to a studio apartment space crunch: hang clothes in an alcove, camouflaged by a pull-down shade. *Right:* A wall-hung trouser rack keeps pants organized and easily accessible in a small space.

Courtesy Lillian Vernon Corp.

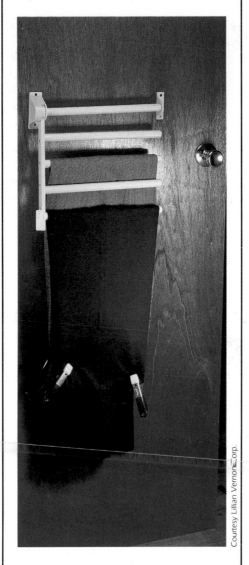

Courtesy Lillian Vernon Corp.

boxes, and sweater boxes. Just because a box says "sweaters" or "shoes" does not mean that you have to store sweaters or shoes in it. Don't forget to use plastic hangers as well as metal skirt and pants hangers. They keep clothing neater and more wrinkle-free than wire hangers and provide a system of organization that is easier to maintain (wire hangers can only be hung in the direction the hook faces, whereas the plastic hanger hook swivels, making it simple to hang everything facing the same direction, which saves space).

Custom closets are the ultimate organizational luxury. But if you can't afford custom, you can achieve the same space-saving, organized results with your own simple additions or with one of the many systems available from companies specializing in interior-organization fixtures for closets.

Hall closets and spare closets offer a particular challenge. Generally chock-a-block full of things such as coats, hats, vacuum cleaners, and skis, they tend to be the dumping ground for things that don't seem to have a final resting place of their own. Once again, look to categories. What do you really want in a closet? Sports gear? Winter coats? Household appliances? If, for example, you decide that you really don't want the skis falling out every time you try to locate an umbrella, perhaps there is another answer.

Courtesy Levelor Lorentzen Inc.

Darryl Baird

Left: **This settee built into a corner saves floor space while creating a cozy conversation nook. With removable cushions and lift-up seats, it also provides storage.**

Courtesy Poggenpohl

Right: By hanging a table upside down from the ceiling, the owner of this kitchen creates convenient storage above the work area where it is most needed.

Right: **The otherwise wasted space of hallway walls can be made functional with cupboards.**

Lynn Karlin

Look for the odd spaces in your apartment that are too small for use as living or entertainment space. Typically, there is space under the stairs, or in a hall corner, or maybe near the entrance to the basement or the attic. In older homes, there is often an extra odd-shaped space on a screened-in back porch, or even in a large bathroom. These odd spaces are ripe for creative storage solutions that make use of the space by closing it off or building attractive cabinetry for storing items out of sight.

After examining and reorganizing your interior storage space, take a look at your exterior shelving. Consider all available wall space in your house or apartment for the possibility of building and installing an attractive and functional wall unit. Either build one yourself or select from the countless combinations available on the market today. You can virtually pick and choose the wall unit you want a section at a time. Wall units hold books, collections, entertainment equipment and accessories, and much more. By adding cabinet fronts to the lower portions of the unit, you can store items that do not necessarily display well, such as papers and toys or games. Large hallways, dens, garages, bedrooms, bathrooms, and even kitchens benefit from shelving of some kind on the walls. It's easy to match any décor with either paint or stain as the finishing touch on your wall unit or shelving.

In fact, if your new storage plans include some redecorating and new furniture, consider items that are functional as well as attractive. End tables with a drawer or shelf are just as attractive as those without. A bed with a bookcase-type headboard provides an area for nighttime reading materials, and bedside tables serve a dual purpose if they include drawer, shelf, or cabinet space below the actual tabletop. Armoires can be used to hold linens, sweaters, and other clothing, as well as toys, games, and hobby materials. Antique sideboards or buffet cabinets can hold records and, in some cases, entertainment equipment. Even filing cabinets now come in traditional finishes to give them a furniture look, so that household files can be stored properly and still be a part of the overall decorative theme.

Containers also provide unlimited organizational solu-

Modular wall units are available for bedrooms, too. Components include shelves, drawers, mini-closets, entertainment centers, and multifunction headboards.

tions for items stored behind cabinet doors or closet doors, as well as items placed in full view. Baskets, bins, trunks, and Plexiglas or lacquered containers hold and organize items while providing an accent to your decorative scheme. Make use of containers for items that always seem to need special storage solutions, such as linens, magazines, papers and files, sewing supplies, hobby materials, and kitchen dry goods, just to name a few. A wicker basket or a trunk with a lid can double, with a piece of glass on top, as a piece of furniture—an end table, bedside table, or coffee table, for example. The interior provides storage for items seldom used, and the exterior provides a nice touch to the décor. Antique trunks also serve nicely as functional furniture, with storage for grandmother's linens or other memorabilia inside. For fishing rods, or other tall items, get an

Multipurpose furniture makes maximum use of a small room. The footlocker/coffee table serves for storage, as do the drawers in the base of the bed/couch. Books, supplies, and the TV are kept out of the way on wall-hung shelves.

architect's bin. A rolling wire-basket system will serve in the closet for everything from underwear to linens to children's games. Use the same basket system in the kitchen for potatoes, onions, and other vegetables. In the den or household "office" area, it converts to hold the household files as well as stationery supplies and stamps for easy access. Give one to the children for their school paperwork and macaroni-art storage. The ideas for storage in baskets, bins, and containers are limitless.

Once you have gone through your belongings and thinned out the excess, categorized what needs to be stored, checked and measured

Left: This pull-out, wire-shelving unit for the kitchen lets you see everything at a glance. Individual shelves can be adjusted to accommodate items of various heights, while accessory grids keep pan lids orderly for easy access.

Right: Closets can be adapted to many other uses: a workshop, darkroom, laundry center, office, greenhouse, or even a dressing room, as shown here.

Courtesy Quaker Maid

the interiors of your existing cabinet and closet space, surveyed any available odd space for potential storage, considered all wall-unit possibilities, and added baskets, bins, containers, and functional furniture to your storage and decorating plans, you are ready to give each room a final walk-through to fine-tune your plans to improve, add to, and maximize your storage space.

Bedroom: Start with the closets; can you double-rod it, add more shelves, install shoe racks, and make use of plastic boxes? Is your bedroom furniture functional? Is there room for a strategically placed wicker or antique trunk (perhaps at the foot of the bed), and do you have under-bed storage containers? Can you add shelves near the bed, or should you add a small bookcase to the room?

Kitchen: Where can you make better use of too deep cabinets with wasted height space? Can you add some shelves and organize the interiors of the cabinets with gadgets and plasticware? Can you put shelving up for cookbooks or spices, and would a rolling basket help you out? If you have a small "office" area in the kitchen, is it organized properly and kept neat? If it isn't, should it be moved to another area of the house?

Hobby Areas: Need a hobby area? Check the attic, garage, basement, and any other extra spaces. Even a large closet can be turned into a small household office center or hobby area.

Children's Rooms: Use the same ideas and techniques for storage in these rooms as you do with the rest of the house. Remember to plan for growth (shelves can hold model airplanes now, records and books later) and to consider the children's ages and heights (a two-year-old cannot handle complicated storage instructions). Also, make sure your organizational and storage plans are simple, so that these rooms will be extra-easy to clean.

Bathroom: See what you can do with your under-sink storage, and don't be afraid to go *up* with wall shelving. Shelves for towels over the commode free up the linen closet for other storage, and guarantee that clean towels are easily accessible for family members and guests.

Now you are more than ready to create, or have someone create for you, the storage space you need for now and into the future.

Much Success!

CHAPTER 2
Basic Storage Concepts and Styles

You need to use your space to its ultimate advantage, and you want it to look good. Once you've assessed your existing storage and determined your needs, it's time to brainstorm options. You can probably come up with several ideas for any given storage snafu, but the trick is in finding the best one. Use your imagination, and don't be afraid of the unconventional—some "farfetched" plans end up being the perfect solutions.

Chapter Three contains many innovative ways to deal with specific storage problems, but for now here are some things to consider.

Open vs. Closed Storage

All homes offer a mixture of storage options: open, or visible, as with bookcases and countertops, and closed, or hidden, as with closets and drawers. Open storage is usually more accessible, so it's good for often-used items. The kitchen is a prime candidate for open storage, since cooking requires so many ingredients and utensils on a regular basis. Open storage also offers the advantage of display—a hand-blown vase deserves to be seen rather than stashed away in a dark cupboard. Even ordinary items such as toys, dishes, home-canned goods, towels, and, of course, books look attractive when arranged on open shelves. On

the other hand, closed storage works well for items you don't necessarily want to look at every day or simply don't use that often. It also offers protection from grime and dust. Some professional organizers feel you shouldn't hang things in the kitchen for that reason. But if you use certain pans, ingredients, and utensils regularly, a little extra dusting of open storage areas is a small price to pay for so much added convenience. As Stephanie Culp says, "If you

Above: Floor-to-ceiling, built-in bookcases can look quite elegant, in addition to saving space. Living room wall storage often combines open and closed treatments. *Above right:* Glass-fronted cabinets offer a compromise in the open versus closed storage debate. Although home maintenance specialists insist these cabinets are hard to keep clean, using a professional squeegee on glass doors will help minimize housework headaches. *Right:* Open storage can be beautiful—like this decorative, built-in wine rack.

don't use it often enough to keep it clean, put it in closed storage!''

Then there's the gray area of cabinets with glass doors: closed storage, in that items are protected from dust, but open to view. Bookcases or shelves, traditionally open storage, can be enclosed simply by attaching hinged shutters or decorative doors. Just remember that anything closed is harder to get to, and thus not as efficient for storing anything in constant use.

One advantage of closed storage is that it doesn't necessarily have to match your decorating scheme. Even if you live in an authentic Georgian town house, you can still use high-tech, space-saving storage units in closets, cabinets, cupboards, and drawers.

Most storage units contain both open and closed space. A prime example is the wall unit, which usually has both shelves and cupboards, and

Courtesy Plain 'n Fancy Kitchens

Courtesy Poggenpohl

Above: Any cupboard will function more efficiently if its contents can be displayed instantly. Hanging bins mounted on cupboard doors allow for easy access.

Left: Although kitchen cabinetry has traditionally featured closed storage, many manufacturers now offer a variety of options—open, closed, and in between.

sometimes has drawers, fold-down desks, and even wet bars. A dresser has a top (open storage) as well as drawers, as do desks, kitchen systems (cabinets and counters), sideboards, etc.

Lifestyle and decorating schemes often determine which options to choose. But generally you'll want the convenience of open storage for the things you use often, and the relative safety of closed storage for everything that can be "out of sight, out of mind," most of the time.

The Logic of Storage: Usage Patterns

The time/motion-study experts agree unanimously: keep things near their point of first use. In other words, if you put on your makeup in the bathroom every morning, that's where it should be stored. If you most often take off your dirty clothes in the bedroom, that's where the hamper belongs. (Some efficiency experts would argue that that's where the washer and dryer belong as well.) If you use your food processor every day, it needs to be within arm's reach. Of course, individual situations will require compromises, but keep the point-of-first-use principle in mind as you decide where you most need additional storage.

Home management specialists also refer to live (or active) vs. dead (or inactive) storage

Courtesy Marvin Windows

Above: **The space under a window seat works well for dead storage. If the space is large, subdivide it into compartments to keep everything in order.**

—anything you use often belongs in live storage, whereas things used only occasionally or seasonally belong in dead storage. These areas are also determined by their location: live storage is easily accessible and fairly central; dead storage is harder to reach and out of the main traffic pattern.

If we apply the point-of-first-use principle here, it's obvious that these areas should be separate. Summer clothes should not be hanging in the closet in the dead of winter; fine crystal

does not belong with the everyday dishes (unless you entertain on a weekly basis!); and toys the children have outgrown do not belong in their rooms.

Since live storage is always "where the action is," it's often given an open treatment. Closed-but-live storage can be multiplied with various features: drawer dividers, pull-out racks, under-the-cabinet appliances, closet systems, etc. Almost every room in your house boasts some live stor-

No matter what your decorating scheme, you'll find storage to match. This antique cupboard enhances the kitchen's country theme, while providing both open and closed storage.

age; look for ways to use it to best advantage.

Some specialists break it down even further, defining dead storage as the area for things that are used only once a year—or never—and adding the term "occasional storage" to describe the area for seasonal paraphernalia. Sports and holiday equipment (fishing poles, ice skates, punch bowls, Christmas-tree ornaments) are put into occasional storage, while old army uniforms, maternity clothes, and grandmother's velvet ottoman are relegated to dead. Maybe because my space is so limited, I think this is getting a little dicey—in a one-bedroom apartment I can't afford to keep much that's NEVER used, and prefer to rotate dead-storage items on a seasonal basis. If you live in a house, however, it may be helpful to distinguish between occasional and dead storage.

The attic, basement, and garage are the typical graveyards of dead storage, as are the top shelves of closets, since they're hard to reach. Boxes, bins, baskets, chests, and even bags are great for dead storage. The drawback, that their contents are inaccessible, hardly matters, since you don't need to get into them but once a year. Clear plastic boxes with lids let you see inside a little better, if that's important, but common sense dictates that dead and/or occasional storage should always be closed.

Also remember that less is more when it comes to inactive storage. (Why do you think they call it dead?) Don't store too many things you have no intention of using. This frees up space for things that you do use occasionally.

Built-in vs. Freestanding Storage Units

Built-in storage can be nothing more than closets, kitchen cabinets, and bookcases, or it can be as specialized as Murphy beds, window seats, and fold-down ironing centers. Though you may not think of them automatically as storage, built-in appliances such as refrigerators, ranges, and dishwashers can save space.

When thinking of remodelling, look for existing space that is not being used within the structure of your house. Architects often square off oddly shaped or tapering areas, and while this looks nice, the space is forever wasted. Prime targets are under stairs, above kitchen cabi-

If you're remodeling or building from scratch, work with a designer to explore built-in storage options. This bibliophile gained a library under the stairs—a space that usually goes to waste.

nets, and under eaves or other architectural features.

The space under stairs can be opened up to house a bookcase, a desk, or simply a small closet. Many kitchens have soffits or headers—a hollow enclosure between the ceiling and the top of the cabinet. This space can be used more efficiently by installing to-the-ceiling cabinets, or simply by opening it up for additional shelves. And closets offer a myriad of possibilities —built-in desks, fold-out hobby centers, Murphy beds, and, in a high-ceilinged home, maybe even a loft bed.

There may be odd space under the eaves of a gable or dormer roof, or where the porch roof attaches to the side of your house, which could be converted to usable storage space. While this mini-closet probably won't be tall, it will have lots of depth and will be good for dead storage of

Storage

Left: Don't overlook the simple, time-honored solutions in your quest for more storage. Utilitarian drawer and shelf units aren't terribly glamorous, but they're an inexpensive way to multiply available space. *Below left:* Freestanding storage furniture is available in every conceivable style and price range, from custom-made cabinetry and Italian designer pieces to department store standards. *Below:* If you're a high-tech cook, an appliance center may be just what you need to get organized. One cabinet houses all your electrical paraphernalia: microwave, coffee maker, toaster, food processor, and mixer, for one-motion storage. *Below right:* Organizational products will help simplify your life. Stairstep shelves keep laundry essentials within easy reach.

things like suitcases, sleeping-bags, skis, golf clubs, and out-of-season clothes.

The corners of rooms are also typically wasted space, but cupboards or shelves can be built in fairly easily. You can even cut into a wall to reveal the space between studs, then install shelves to create shallow, built-in bookcases, cupboards, knickknack shelves, or a fold-out ironing center.

Remodelling or building from scratch gives you lots of

leeway. So in the initial planning stages at least, let your imagination run wild and see what comes up. I heard of a man who built his house out in the country and created a rolling kitchen island with two stainless-steel sinks and counter space; he used a length of flexible pipe so the island could roll over to the stove or cabinets when he was cooking intensively. While this idea might not appeal to some people—and

might not be allowed by local building codes—in this man's rustic, backwoods kitchen, where his cabinets and island are made of old barn wood, it really works.

One warning about building more storage: don't let your changes look tacked on, or like afterthoughts. They must work harmoniously with the existing space. Get professional help from a reputable designer, architect, or contractor, or, if doing it yourself, think everything all the way through with plans on paper. Don't rush into anything. Consider the scale of the room as a whole, and the relationship between your project and the furniture you will place in the room. You'll have to live with your "improvements" for a long time, so make sure they really are just that.

You may feel restricted to freestanding components either by budget or because you rent, but they have some advantages. You can take them with you when you move and rearrange them as furniture in the meantime. You can also build storage without knocking down walls. The most common way is to hang shelves, but you could even convert a closet—there are fasteners and joining devices available that allow you to install fold-out desks and shelves and remove them later, with just screw holes to fill. (On page 98 there are plans for converting a closet without even drilling holes in the wall.)

One of the great new waves in freestanding storage

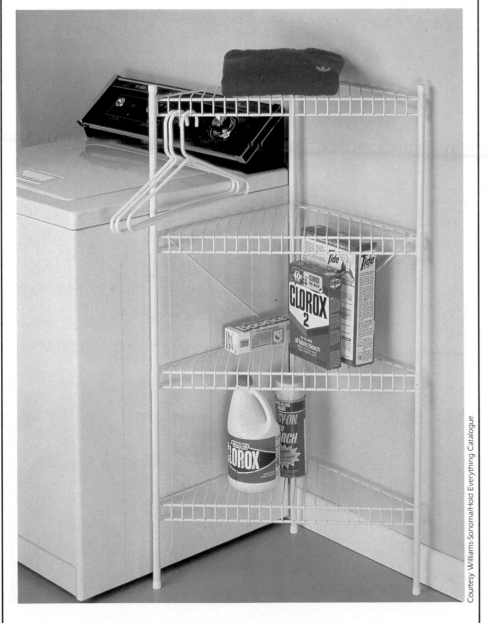

is knock-down (KD) furniture —ready-to-assemble units that come in what look like giant pizza boxes. They can be put together and taken apart with a screwdriver or allen wrench, and though you'll save money by doing it yourself, many dealers will assemble units for a small charge.

Most KD furniture is imported from Scandinavia and Germany, and dealers say that being able to ship and store it unassembled represents a sav-

ings for both the store and the customer. Because it's often modular, you can buy various pieces at different times and know they'll work together. Best of all, almost everything imaginable is available as KD: platform beds with built-in nightstands as well as headboards and under-bed storage; component wall units, entertainment centers, and bookcases; computer desks and office equipment with optional typing carriages, file

Under-the-cabinet appliances free up valuable counter space. Some models even feature built-in lights to brighten the work area.

drawers, and lap drawers; kids' bunk beds, trundle beds, and work stations; even dining-room and kitchen tables with self-storing leaves.

But remember, whether you plan to buy or to build additional storage, the first step is always to measure your available space, taking into account all protrusions and obstacles, such as pipes, baseboards, windows, doors, and furniture. Furniture salespeople are amazed at how many customers have no idea how

big a space they're working with—do your part to disprove the stereotype!

Space Savers

Besides the multifunctional furniture and various cabinet and closet systems on the market today, many appliances are now designed to save space by storing more efficiently. There are under-shelf models of microwaves, coffee makers,

Children who share a small bedroom will gain more living space with a trundle or bunk bed. And remember that wall units are for kids, too!

Right: A Murphy bed allows you to use the same space for sleeping and living without sacrificing style.

Below: Wall units are the ultimate space-saver, accommodating everything but the kitchen sink.

Courtesy Techline/By Marshall Erdman and Associates, Inc.

free-lancing from my apartment, I worked in the living room because that's where my desk had always been. But it seemed awfully silly to have the bedroom lie fallow all day while my work engulfed the rest of the house, so I bought a futon frame and moved the bed into the living room to act as a couch by day. Now my office is in the "bedroom," and I sleep in the living room.

Decorating

No matter what your decorating scheme, there are lots of compatible storage options. For instance, oak cabinets, cedar chests, woven baskets, and wooden pegs or cast-iron configurations will enhance a traditional or country look. High-tech styles abound: modular, stacking storage units in sleek plastics; vinyl-coated steel-rod shelving, racks, drawer systems, and carts; full-length laminated wall units with a place for everything from a TV and stereo system to books and knick-knacks.

There is also multi-functional furniture to match just about any décor. Daybeds and hide-a-beds are obvious examples. They've been available for years in a variety of designs and fabrics. You can even find Shaker-style convertible beds, built to order by Kipp and Margot Osborne of Wooden Furniture, in New York City. Wall units come in traditional styles as well as modern, and cabinets run the

Courtesy Plain 'n Fancy Kitchens

toasters—even TVs—as well as under-the-sink dishwashers, compact ranges, space-saving refrigerators, and trash compactors.

Stackable washers and dryers are another excellent example of space-saving appliances. Some are only 24 inches wide and will fit into standard closets, so you can apply the point-of-first-use rule and have your "laundry room" in the bathroom or bedroom. Even putting it in the kitchen, workshop, family room, or hall closet will probably save steps. The only restrictions are access to plumbing and electrical or gas hookups, and outside venting for the dryer.

Another way to save space is to reexamine the function of a room, because sometimes it'll do double duty. The living room can also be the guest room, the kitchen might harbor an office, and a well-placed wall unit can function as a room divider. For instance, when I first started

Check into the variety of ready-to-assemble storage furniture on the market. You'll find models to suit every taste, often in a multitude of colors. These tubular steel shelves, for instance, are available in 20 different hues.

aren't absolutely bound to your decorating scheme. The right antique chest could work in a stark, minimalist décor, and old-fashioned copper pans might be handsomely displayed on a high-tech rack in an otherwise country kitchen. Be aware of your over-all decorating scheme, but, don't be afraid to break with convention.

Shelves

Shelves are the universal storage receptacles. They can be put up just about anywhere—in any room, in closets, under sinks, and even on the backs of doors. They can be free-standing or mounted to the wall, open or closed, strictly horizontal or with vertical dividers. Stair-step shelves can be used to display spices or bath supplies in deep, dark cabinets.

The most convenient do-it-yourself shelving is the metal track-and-bracket type, available at any hardware store. But when you're up against a hollow wall (sheetrock, drywall, plasterboard or wallboard), always attach the shelves directly to studs. Don't risk an accident—a wonderful new storage receptacle that promptly falls down is not just inconvenient, it's humiliating and sometimes dangerous.

Studs are usually sixteen inches apart from center to center, but this may vary occasionally. The traditional way of finding them is to rap the wall

gamut from wood to onyx laminate. Rolling utility carts can be made of anything from polypropylene to glass, from anodized aluminum to finely crafted walnut.

The execution of any given design is what determines its compatibility to a particular decorating style. To oversimplify a bit, modern has flat, unbroken surfaces, made of synthetic materials, while traditional often features ornamented surfaces of natural materials. Of course, you with your knuckles until you hear a "solid" sound, but you can also buy an inexpensive magnetic stud-finder. Or you can measure sixteen inches from a corner, and most likely you'll find a stud.

If the studs don't fall where you need them, use molly or toggle bolts, which fan out behind the drywall, locking the bolt into place. These fasteners distribute weight over a large area and will hold fairly heavy loads. However, use several of them at key spots or you may end up with a mess on your floor instead of shelves on the wall.

For hanging shelves on brick, concrete, or cinder-block walls, you'll need a lead anchor and a drill with a carbide bit. Make a deep hole in the mortar that's wide enough to accept the plug, but not too big or the plug won't hold. Screw a bolt into the plug to attach your shelves to the wall.

Shelves come in all shapes and sizes, and provide storage space in every room of the house. Roll-out bins make deep shelves more efficient.

Modular Wall System-Eurodesign Ltd./Room Design: Lou Middleton Interiors, Cupertino, Calif.

A STEP-BY-STEP GUIDE
PROJECT 1
The Basic Shelf

Planning is the first step. Settle on the length, depth, and width needed for what you're going to store. Also consider the weight the shelf will be supporting—will it simply be light knickknacks or heavy hardback books? Heavier loads need to be anchored to wall studs, while lighter loads can be toggle-bolted to wallboard.

Building-supply stores or lumber stores have assorted lumber sizes, but remember that board measurements refer to size before the wood is milled. A 1 x 6 may really measure ¾" x 5½".

A very simple knickknack shelf is used here for illustration; you can adjust the dimensions to fit your needs.

For the top and bottom, cut two pine 1 x 4s two feet long. Cut two pine 1 x 4s 18" long for the sides. Make sure the boards are cut very straight— butt joints need a good square cut in order to look good. Use a square; for best results use a hand-held circular saw or a jigsaw set at 90 degrees. If sawing by hand, use steady pressure and follow your guideline carefully.

Being careful to line up the boards at right angles, with the sides lapping both top and bottom shelves, glue and screw the top and bottom to the sides. (Screws hold better than nails—they have more bite and can't be pulled out. If you use a countersink bit on the drill, the screws will fit flush with the wood.) Use a

SCREWS
(TYPICAL)

¼" PLYWOOD BACK FLUSH FOUR SIDES.
GLUE AND NAIL ALL AROUND.

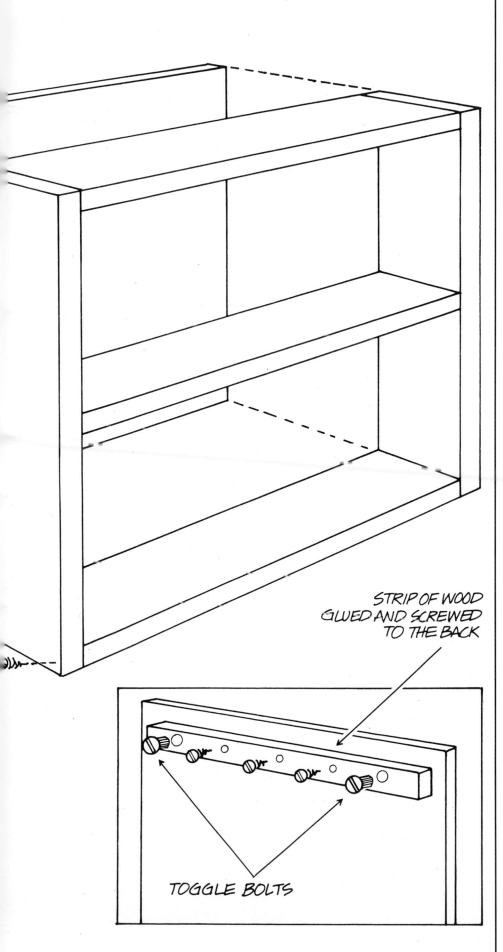

STRIP OF WOOD
GLUED AND SCREWED
TO THE BACK

TOGGLE BOLTS

carpenter's square to square the corners.

Measure the distance between the two sides, and cut a pine 1 x 4 to this length for the middle shelf. Glue and screw into place using light pencil guidelines to show where to position it before the final fastening.

Using ¼" plywood, cut a back that fits flush on all four sides. Glue and screw a 1 x 2 cut to the same length as the middle shelf ¾" from the top (just below where the top shelf will be); this will be used to hang the shelves. Drill two holes 2" from each end to accommodate toggle bolts. Firmly attach the back to the rest of the shelf using glue and nails or screws. Sixteen 1" nails placed evenly around the back should be enough to hold the load.

Sandpaper the entire work and finish to your liking, being careful to paint or varnish all sides. (If you leave the back unfinished, moisture can get in and cause the boards to warp over time.)

Place the shelf against the wall where you plan to hang it, and level it carefully by eye or with a carpenter's level. Make pencil marks through the holes onto the wall to provide a guide for drilling. Drill the holes to accept the toggle bolts and hang the shelf.

For a fancier version, use a higher grade of wood and fasten with dowel pins. You could also apply moldings or 1 x 2s on the front to frame in the shelves (and cover up any sloppy saw work).

CHAPTER 3
Specific Storage Problems and Their Solutions

Kitchens

Dissatisfaction with kitchens runs high. The "heart of the home" is the room most often remodelled—Americans spend $17.8 billion annually redoing their kitchens. Inefficient work areas, inadequate counter and cabinet space, lack of electrical outlets, and poor lighting and ventilation are the most frequent problems. The kitchen is often a multifunctional room where

An efficient kitchen design allows for adequate storage, light, and ventilation near each of the work centers.

Courtesy Quaker Maid

Above: **The kitchen should reflect your culinary style. If baking is a high priority, consider setting aside space solely for this purpose. Keep all of your ingredients and utensils there, and invest in wall-mounted cooling racks.**

food is not only stored and prepared, but eaten; where schedules are planned and bills paid; where family and friends can get together informally for a chat and a cup of coffee. It's bound to fall short in one of these areas!

The needs of an efficiency kitchen are quite different from the needs of one used to cook elaborate gourmet meals; so the first step is to establish your priorities. For instance, if you do a lot of baking you need a convenient place for pie, cake, and bread pans, special utensils, and the electric mixer, but if you rarely bake, this paraphernalia doesn't deserve prime space. If you entertain often, your fine china, crystal, table linens, and silver should be easily ac-

cessible. If you have company only a couple of times a year, on holidays, your stemware could be stored on the very top shelf of the cupboard. If you do your own canning, you'll need easy access to the mason jars, paraffin, and pressure cooker during the summer, though they may be in dead storage the rest of year.

Also consider your shopping patterns. Do you stockpile staples when there's a sale? Buy soft drinks or beer by the six-pack or case? Serve mostly fresh foods, rather than frozen or canned? Your answers will determine where you need storage the most.

Think about what's working—and what isn't. Do you feel like you're running an obstacle course whenever you try to fix dinner? Are your tools where you need them, when you need them? Tailor your storage system to your own cooking style and architectural circumstances, but remember the point-of-first-use principle and store things you use often within easy reach.

The Work Centers

Time/motion experts emphasize the work triangle—the triangle formed between your sink, stove, and refrigerator. Think of each point as being a separate work center, and store the things you use there. Think about how you operate in your kitchen, and what's going to be most convenient for YOU.

For instance, the sink is the designated cleanup center—not just for dishes but also for fruits and vegetables. Keep things such as the cutting board, paring knives, and colander nearby, as well as the obvious scouring pads, dish detergent, and cleaning supplies. Everyday dishes and glassware are also most often stored near the sink or dishwasher so they're easy to put away. Space permitting, also store anything that's first filled with water—teapot, saucepans, coffee pot—near the sink. However, when arranging your kitchen, be sure to leave 24" on either side of the sink to use as a work area.

The range is the cooking center, so keep pots and pans, pot holders, condiments, large

Brian Leatart

spoons, tongs, and other cooking utensils within easy reach. As with the sink, the ideal is to have 24" of counter space on either side of the cooking surface, but this is seldom a reality.

The refrigerator is the storage center, and in many kitchens an adjacent counter serves for food preparation. Ideally this counter affords 18" of work space on the side that the refrigerator door opens. (If this counter is also adjacent to the sink, however, it should be

at least 36" long.) Storing your nonperishable foods in a cabinet near the refrigerator will save time when putting away the groceries. A bigger kitchen may afford a separate preparation center, where you could store small appliances, cookbooks, canisters, mixing bowls, and utensils.

For optimum efficiency, the total steps between all three points of the work triangle should be no more than 22 feet and no less than 12 feet. If your kitchen doesn't measure

Left: In a large kitchen with separated work centers, an island may be the best way to increase efficiency. (It also enables two cooks to work at the same time without getting in each other's way.) *Below:* A well-organized cooking center will increase your joy of cooking. Strive for one-motion storage of everything you use on a regular basis. *Right:* Look for multifunctional products for the kitchen, too. This spice rack does double duty for dish towel and pot holder storage.

Below: Food processor blades can be stored, in a pocketed holder for safety and instant access. *Right:* If Chinese stir-fry is your passion, provide open storage for your wok and related utensils. *Far right:* Utensils can make an attractive "bouquet" when clustered together in a sturdy vase or crock.

up, don't despair. Stephanie Culp suggests you set up a work station in the center of the room—there are islands on casters and modular islands made of banks of stacking drawers, as well as built-in units that fold out to triple the workspace (manufactured by Armstrong World Industries). A rolling utility cart with a butcher-block top or a fold-down table is a good compromise for a small space. Many kitchens, however, don't have enough space for two people to stand, let alone for a work island. Throughout this section there are ways to better use any available space.

In her book, *Escape from the Kitchen,* Deniece Schofield outlines four storage principles that will help organize any work center.

The first principle we've already talked about: store things where they are first used. The second is equally simple: store things with motion in mind. The prime spots are between hip and eye level—you can reach in and grab things quickly, and they're just as easy to put back. You're aiming for what Deniece calls one-motion storage for anything you use on a regular basis.

The third principle is to store things in well-defined, well-confined places. Drawer dividers are a lifesaver here, as are some of the other organizing gadgets. When "everything is in its place," you can lay your hands on the garlic press or tea ball at a moment's notice. Always store items that are used together in the same place—you shouldn't have to hike across the kitchen to find the food-processor blades.

The fourth principle relates back to number three: label. Nothing is more frustrating than to have a well-defined, well-confined place for something and then find it's missing. Deniece suggests you label the drawer dividers as to what belongs where—that way everyone knows.

Judc Pilossof

Cooking Tools and Supplies

If your work centers are far apart, consider buying duplicates of often used utensils. That little extra expense may save miles in the long run.

If you prefer closed storage, store cooking tools in a nearby drawer, using dividers to keep everything organized and easily accessible. Out in the open, they can be corralled in ceramic jars, or suspended from a wall grid. Grids vary from a

simple pegboard to more elaborate Colonial or industrial styles. You can make your own wooden grid by simply nailing strips of lath to a frame (lath are the thin, narrow strips of wood used in construction as a groundwork for plaster or tile) and using S-hooks for hanging kitchen tools.

Wall-mounted magnetic racks are great for knives, scissors, and small metal utensils, but beware of loading them up with heavy knives. They may hold at first, but could be

jarred loose later—as you're chopping onions nearby, for instance—and that's dangerous. Lightweight, nonlethal tools such as strainers, graters, corkscrews, bottle openers, and peelers are perfect for a magnetic rack, as are a *few* knives. Common sense is the key here.

A safer, if bulkier, alternative for knife storage is the knife block. Also, hanging knife racks can be attached to a wall or the side of a base cabinet for storage in otherwise

In addition to providing convenient open storage, wall grids may also add visual interest by combining different colors, textures, and shapes.

wasted space. Knife blocks and racks are popular do-it-yourself projects you can make out of everything from scrap lumber to mahogany, maple, or pine. Or, if you have a butcher-block counter or work island, simply cut slots in the work surface for use as a knife rack.

If you have an overabundance of drawer space, consider creating a specialized cutlery drawer with a grooved strip for holding knives in place. Some cabinet manufacturers feature these as part of their line, but they're easy to make yourself. Just cut grooves in a board that fits the width of your drawer, then glue it in place.

Hang pots and pans on a wall rack or overhead on a suspended grid. If you're worried about dust or dislike the look of open storage, hang your pans on the back of a door, or install a slide-out pan rack in a base cupboard near the stove. You can either make these yourself, with pegboard, S-hooks, and drawer slides, or

Brian Leatart

Courtesy Poggenpohl

Courtesy Ralph Wilson Plastics Company

buy one of the many commercial varieties.

Plates and glassware are usually stored near the sink or dishwasher for one-motion storage, though some people prefer to keep them near the eating area. Depending on the shape of your cabinet space, you may want to purchase either the "stand up" organizers, where the plates fit into slots and are lined up vertically, or the stacking "in/out basket" type for low, horizontal spaces. These tiered racks add space while they organize your dishes. There are also under-shelf racks for suspending stemware upside down.

Think about how often you use your small appliances vs. the space they occupy. Under-the-shelf models of toasters, toaster ovens, coffee makers, can openers, and microwaves free up valuable counter space. NuTone manufactures a motor that, installed under a countertop, will run twelve appliances—everything from a can opener, food processor, or blender to a meat grinder,

Left: Compact built-in appliances save steps as well as space. *Above left:* Pullout cupboard organizers make it a cinch to keep "everything in its place." *Right:* If you're desperately low on counter space, multiply your work area with a cutting board designed to sit over the sink. This one also has a strainer for draining wet fruits and vegetables.

ice crusher, or knife sharpener. When not in use, the appliances can be stowed away in slide-out trays installed in base cabinets.

A more homespun way to increase counter space is to take a hard look at your canisters — and whatever else is currently occupying the all-important work area. Maybe you aren't ready to run out and buy an under-shelf microwave, but meanwhile you could suspend the flour, sugar, coffee, and tea canisters under the cabinet. Or, if you use a dish drainer, get one designed to hang over the sink. Second choice would be a folding one (made either of wood or vinyl-coated steel) that can be put away with the dishes. If counter space is at a real premium but there's no room for a utility cart, use one of those cutting boards made to fit over the sink. Sturdy pull-out breadboards are another way to extend your counter

space. Or you can improvise work space by cutting a piece of wood to fit on top of a drawer. Design the board with slides so it will store inside the drawer.

Cookbooks can be stored spine-up in a deep drawer, in a magazine-type rack on the wall, or on a special shelf. When hanging shelves for cookbooks, be sure to use the right kind of fasteners (see Chapter Two), because books exert quite a load—hardbacks weigh an average of 25 pounds per square foot. If your cookbook collection is extensive but you're tight on space, consider keeping only your favorites in the kitchen; store the more exotic or special-occasion books in the living-room bookcase.

As for recipe files, Stephanie Culp recommends keeping them between clear plastic sheet protectors in a three-ring binder. Recipes printed on only one side of a page can be stapled to the black construction-paper insert; for recipes

Storing spices in a cool, dark drawer near the stove keeps them accessible and protects their flavor and longevity.

mounted racks, under-cabinet, pull-down spice caddies, vinyl-coated steel shelves attached to the inside of cabinet doors, square revolving spice racks that hold 24 standard-sized cans, expandable stair-step shelves, specialty cabinets with swing-out shelves, and more. Deniece Schofield keeps her spices in alphabetical order in a shallow drawer, tops labelled with black Magic Marker. Which system you pick will depend on how often you use spices and whether you're willing to spend a little extra time cleaning for the convenience of open storage.

Kitchen Storage Spaces

If you have a pantry, there are deluxe swing-out shelf units that multiply your space and make food retrieval easier. While these are usually top of the line, custom-built jobs, you can find similar units ready to install on the backs of cabinet doors. Pull-out shelves are a less expensive alternative, but, in any case, avoid stacking cans or boxes on top of one another, or you'll constantly be shuffling them around when you go to find something.

Corner cupboards are traditionally wasted space because they're so deep and dark, but with lazy-Susan shelves you can open them up and "let the sun shine in." These are different from lazy Susans that simply sit on a shelf—these are actual shelves that rotate on a

printed on both sides of a page, remove the insert and staple them directly to the clear plastic. Keep categories separate with tab dividers, or, if your recipe file is really extensive, keep categories in different notebooks. Culp stresses that you should never clip recipes unless you really intend to try them; throw them away if you haven't tried them within a few weeks.

There are almost as many ways to store spices as there are kinds of spices—wall-pole. Lazy-Susan shelves are featured in many cabinet lines, as well as in closet-organization systems. If you don't install one, use this dead zone for storing little-used equipment such as the ice-cream maker, turkey-roasting pan, eggnog cups, or fondue pot. (If you haven't made fondue in years, however, your favorite charity could probably put the thing to better use.) Obviously, if your kitchen space is really tight, these once-a-year items should be banished to the hinterlands of the basement, attic, or storage bin.

Cupboards over the refrigerator or built-in range are also notoriously hard to reach. Some newer homes have vertical shelves for trays and cookie sheets built-in here; another option is a built-in wine rack. If your cupboard lacks these amenities and you don't feel like adding them, use this space for dead storage. In a pinch, it can be your backup pantry for duplicate items you haven't quite run out of—paper towels, catsup, molas-

ses, cereal, etc. A lazy Susan provides easier access, while sacrificing a little corner space.

A wastebasket near the sink will facilitate cleanup. Some people put it under the sink, but this can be rather awkward. Trash racks that attach to the inside of the cabinet door keep trash easy to reach but out of sight; however, because they aren't usually covered, you will need to empty them more often to keep odors down.

Cleaning supplies are often stored under the sink or in a broom closet. No matter where they end up, keep waxes, polishes, detergents, sponges, scrub brushes, etc. in a plastic or wire basket that can be carried anywhere in the house. Hang brooms, mops, and polishers from hooks in a small closet or on an inconspicuous wall (above the basement stairs, or in the space between the wall and the refrigerator, for instance).

Creating Space

Focusing on the work centers, look for ways to use currently wasted space. Again, shelves are the great universal storage device—you can convert a closet to a walk-in pantry by lining it with shelves, add shelves to the ends of cabinets, or suspend shelves from the ceiling for plants, baskets, pottery, etc. Hooks, racks, and grids can be used to store everything from cleaning sup-

Courtesy Poggenpohl

Left: This cabinet combines an open-out pantry, wine rack, and deep drawers to make maximum use of a small space. *Below:* Lazy-Susan shelves are best for transforming those dark corner cupboards into usable storage space. *Right:* Thin base cabinets work well for storing cookie sheets and bread boards.

Courtesy Ralph Wilson Plastics Company

Left: Built-in shelves offer one-motion storage in this kitchen.

Brian Leatart

plies to cooking utensils.

With a few modifications, the false front directly below your sink can be converted to a tilt out storage bin or shallow shelf for holding scouring pads, sponges, and soap. Or consider knocking out the space between studs in one of your walls and installing a broom closet, cookbook library, or additional storage.

If you're in the market for new appliances, look for compact combination models that do two jobs in the space of one—a combination microwave and electric range that occupies only a 30"-wide space, for instance.

And take advantage of "automatic organizers" to multiply your available storage: pull-out bins, slide-out baskets, and swing-out shelves can be installed with just a hand drill and a screwdriver. Check out the freestanding components, too: hanging wire baskets for storing potatoes, onions, ap-

ples, or whatever; utensil caddies and knife blocks; drawer dividers and flatware trays. You'll find complete organizing systems at hardware, home-center, and department stores, in mail-order catalogues and specialty stores. Think about what you need, then go on a browsing or research expedition. The array of products available may seem overwhelming, so don't buy anything until you've shopped around a bit. You want to make a smart choice.

Organize your kitchen for total efficiency by planning for your individual usage patterns. Always position storage as close as possible to "the point of first use."

A STEP-BY-STEP GUIDE
PROJECT 2
Space-Saving Pantry

If you're tired of crouching down and fumbling around in the deep space of under-counter cabinets, this project will make retrieval a much more pleasant experience.

Before you start, you may need to remove an existing shelf. If it's fixed with dado joints, use a saber saw to cut a wide V into the shelf, with the point of the V at the back. When the V drops out, the other pieces can be pulled from the dadoes.

Next, determine the dimensions of what you'll be storing. For instance, if you plan to store canned goods, measure the largest can to figure how wide you'll need to make each drawer; add 1" for the shelf lip. If you want to hang pots and pans, measure your deepest pan and divide this dimension into the total width of your cabinet.

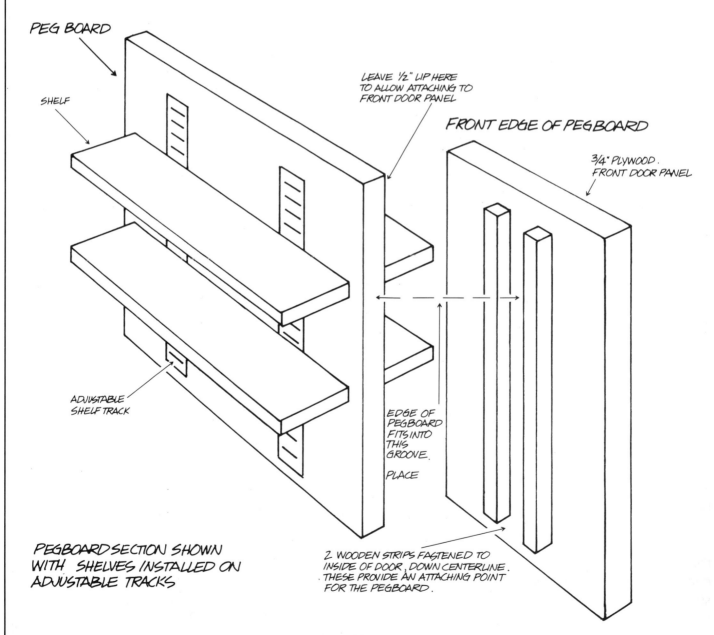

PEG BOARD

SHELF

LEAVE ½" LIP HERE
TO ALLOW ATTACHING TO
FRONT DOOR PANEL

FRONT EDGE OF PEGBOARD

3/4" PLYWOOD.
FRONT DOOR PANEL

ADJUSTABLE
SHELF TRACK

EDGE OF
PEGBOARD
FITS INTO
THIS
GROOVE.

PLACE

PEGBOARD SECTION SHOWN
WITH SHELVES INSTALLED ON
ADJUSTABLE TRACKS

2 WOODEN STRIPS FASTENED TO
INSIDE OF DOOR, DOWN CENTERLINE.
THESE PROVIDE AN ATTACHING POINT
FOR THE PEGBOARD.

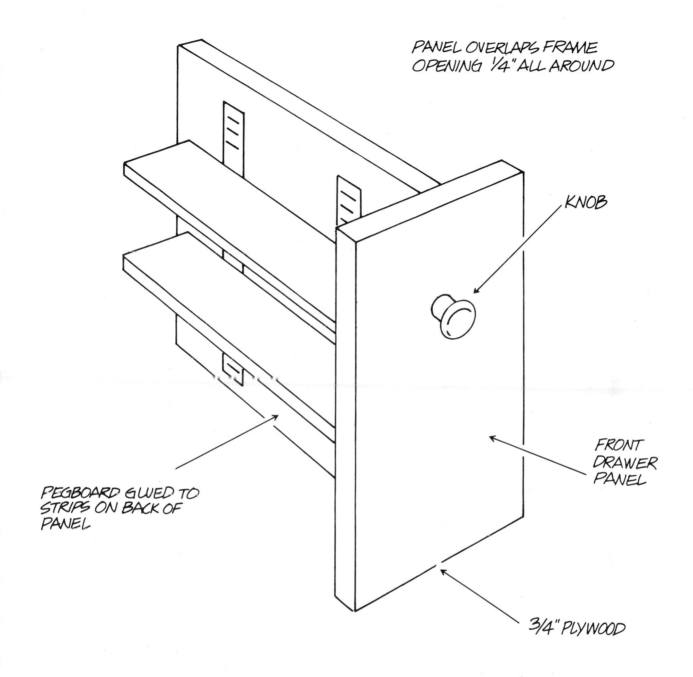

PANEL OVERLAPS FRAME
OPENING ¼" ALL AROUND

KNOB

PEGBOARD GLUED TO
STRIPS ON BACK OF
PANEL

FRONT
DRAWER
PANEL

¾" PLYWOOD

Shop at your building-supply store for telescoping drawer slides to fill the depth. Install the slides on top and bottom in the center of each space allowed for drawers.

Use tempered pegboard for the drawers; cut sections for each drawer, allowing for the space taken up by the top and bottom tracks. Each pegboard section should be 2" less than the depth of the space, to allow for the front panel and knob. Install pegboard in track, making sure it rolls smoothly.

Attach track-and-bracket shelving to pegboard for shelves, making sure it's bolted through brackets. Add a lip to shelves by nailing 1 x 2s along the edges.

Cut the door panels from ¾" plywood. Attach two wooden strips to the inside of each door to provide a groove for the pegboard; glue into place. Add a knob to the outside of the drawer.

A STEP-BY-STEP GUIDE
PROJECT 3
Movable Work Island with Butcher-Block Top

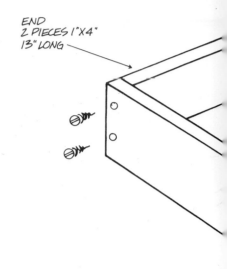

END
2 PIECES 1"X4"
13" LONG

Build a frame of 1 x 4s: two 13" pieces butted by two 25" pieces. (You may alter these dimensions to suit your preference.) Screw and glue frame into place; it will be used to support the butcher-block work surface.

Cut four 32" legs from 2 x 2 stock. Drill holes in the bottoms to accept 2" casters. (The casters and the top will bring the height to about 36"—the standard working-counter height.) Glue and screw legs to frame. To brace the legs, cut four wedges from 2 x 4 stock; screw and glue into corners. Cut a 2 x 4 to fit snugly between the legs at the ends; glue and screw into place from the inside.

Construct the top of 2 x 2s; any wood will do, but maple is best because it's hard. Make it big enough to overlap the supporting frame by 1" on all sides. Drill three holes in each 2 x 2 in exactly the same place; use a drill press if possible. Apply glue and insert dowel rods; you could also use threaded steel rods, then plug with ¾" plugs. Clamp and allow to dry overnight.

Position the top so there's 1" overlap on all sides. Apply glue around the frame where it meets the butcher block. Clamp firmly and allow to dry. With clamps still in place, drill screw holes in frame at an angle. Use 12 screws to fasten the frame into the bottom side

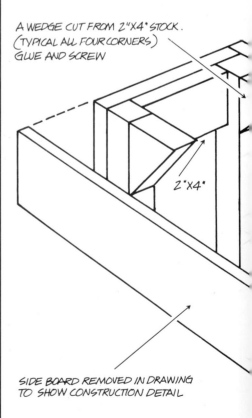

A WEDGE CUT FROM 2"X4" STOCK.
(TYPICAL ALL FOUR CORNERS)
GLUE AND SCREW

2"X4"

SIDE BOARD REMOVED IN DRAWING
TO SHOW CONSTRUCTION DETAIL

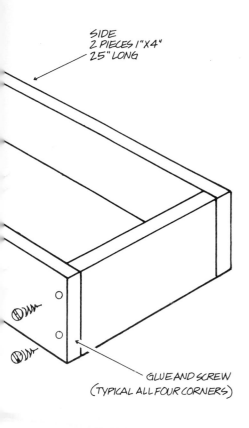

SIDE
2 PIECES 1"X4"
25" LONG

GLUE AND SCREW
(TYPICAL ALL FOUR CORNERS)

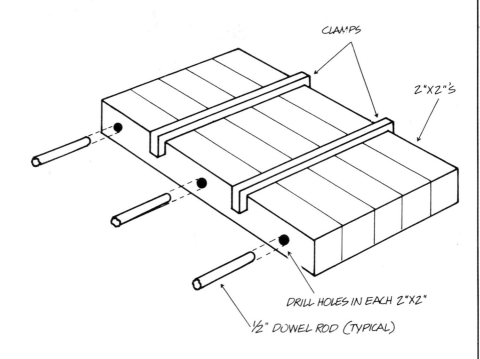

CLAMPS

2"X2"'S

DRILL HOLES IN EACH 2"X2"

½" DOWEL ROD (TYPICAL)

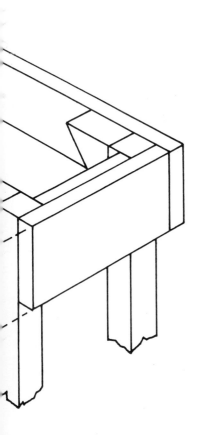

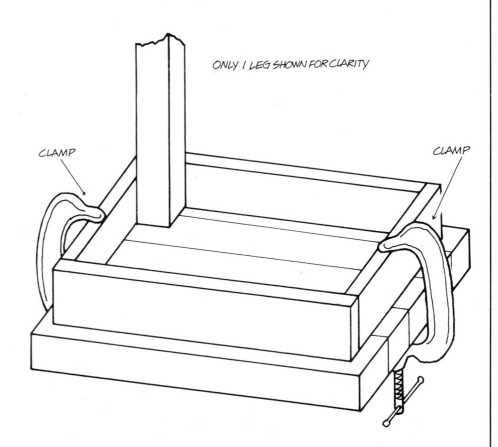

ONLY 1 LEG SHOWN FOR CLARITY

CLAMP

CLAMP

of the top, taking care that they only penetrate partway through the top.

Cut two shelves from ¾" plywood; laminate them together, then notch corners to fit around legs. Apply strips of veneer all around to dress up exposed plywood edges. Drill countersink holes, screw shelves into place. Fill holes with wood putty and sand.

Attach casters following manufacturer's instructions. Plane down any uneven spots on the top; sand and apply Behlen's oil or vegetable oil to butcher block. Sand the rest of the table and stain, varnish, or paint entire base of table. Apply several coats and lightly sand in between applications. Finally, apply a sealer and two or more coats of varnish.

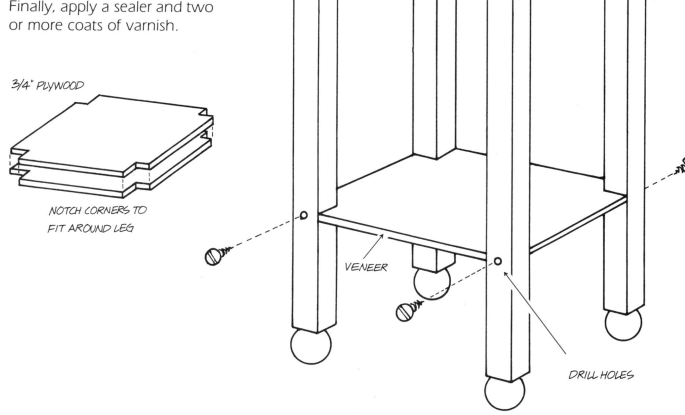

3/4" PLYWOOD

NOTCH CORNERS TO
FIT AROUND LEG

VENEER

DRILL HOLES

Bedrooms

Like kitchens, bedrooms present a unique storage challenge in that they, too, are often multifunctional—you read in bed, watch TV, pay the bills at a small desk in the corner, iron clothes; kids' rooms often double as play-rooms. Since bedrooms also function as dressing rooms, this is where clothes are usually stored—too often in a closet that's a disaster zone.

So once again, your first question is "What is the room used for?" If you read in bed, you'll need a place for books and a good light. As for watching TV, maybe investing in a cabinet that holds not only the television but also contains drawers for storing shirts, underwear, or socks would be a good idea. If your house is old, you may have an inefficient, deep closet in the bedroom which could be re-modelled into a custom wall

Wall units can be used in bedrooms to multiply available storage space. Custom-designed systems will accommodate windows, doors, fireplaces, and other architectural features.

unit with a smaller closet, shelves, drawers, and a built-in desk. Studio-apartment dwellers may want to use a hide-a-bed, a convertible futon frame, or even a Murphy bed to effectively store the bed during the daytime. Think about what's working and what isn't, then look for answers to your individual problems. Let's start with that nearly universal complaint, the closet.

Closets

No matter how much closet space is available, there never seems to be enough room for a new dress or another suit. This is partly because the standard pole-and-shelf arrangement of most closets wastes a lot of space, and because most people tend to accumulate too many clothes. According to Stephanie Culp, the first step for clearing out closet clutter is to take everything out of the closet and get rid of all the clothes you haven't worn in two years, as well as any garment that's ''too small, too dated, too faded, torn and not fixable, not wearable because it doesn't go with anything, or just not you.'' Then you're ready to convert wasted space into usable storage.

Closet systems are the easiest way to transform your existing space. There are quite a few on the market, both custom-built and ready-to-assemble units. If you're handy, you can invent one yourself. Most feature a dou-

Closet shelf organizers keep everything in a well-defined place.

Courtesy Lillian Vernon Corp.

ble rod so you can hang twice as many skirts, shirts, and jackets in the same space; they may also include shelves, drawers, cubbyholes, and pull-out bins, as well as accessory organizers for shoes, belts, and ties. Closet systems can double your available storage space and provide easy access for all your clothing and accessories, so they're definitely worth the investment.

Professional organizer Linda London stresses the individualistic nature of closets. "You need to take into account the type of clothing, accessories, and even the type of person who's using the closet. A man who wears suspenders and owns 55 pairs will want them instantly retrievable; a woman who wears a lot of bulky sweaters will need a different set-up from someone who wears tailored suits."

For starters, hang your clothes by category—separate dresses, jackets, slacks, shirts, blouses, etc. Culp suggests you also arrange articles within each category by palette to make it easier and quicker to coordinate outfits. You can break the categories down even further: work blouses in one section, sport or casual tops in another; evening dresses apart from everyday dresses. Having specific spaces for everything will help you overcome any tendency toward slob syndrome.

London recommends prioritizing your wardrobe, then placing your most important items in the most visible and easily accessible part of your closet. For instance, if you love dresses and wear them more than anything else, put them in the front of the closet. Or if you dress from the feet up and hate bending over, keep shoes on shelves from knee to waist height.

Maxine Ordesky, a Beverly Hills-based professional organizer, offers these tips for redoing your closet. "Measure the horizontal space (how many feet of blouses, slacks, etc.) and vertical dimensions (from hanger to hem) of all categories of clothes. Then plan your sections for double hanging.

For instance, if your longest skirt is 39", put the rod 41" from the floor. And let's say your longest blouse is 34"—put your top rod 36" up from the bottom one. Then increase your space allowance by category. If you now have two horizontal feet of blouses but want more, allow for three feet." Ordesky says that most people look only at width and depth, ignoring vertical space that could be put to good use.

If your closet is extremely small, you need to utilize every available inch. Look to the side walls, back wall, door, and floor. London works mainly in Manhattan, where "closets are like cheeseboxes —and so are the bedrooms!" She'll sometimes grid an entire wall in narrow closets, with hooks for hanging belts, scarves, robes, suspenders, clothes, and even shoes. She'll also knock down the partition between two long and deep

Below: **Wire stacking baskets are great for closet storage. They are space efficient, relatively inexpensive, and allow for free airflow around clothes.**

Above: **Some closet rods feature attached hangers and hanger extensions. By alternating heights of hanging clothes, these systems help keep clothes from getting crushed.**

only see half your wardrobe at one time, and folding doors eliminate usable wall space on either side of the closet. If your closet has either of these kinds of doors, consider replacing them with ones that open and shut, or simply remove the doors and hang blinds or curtains as coverups. Or you could leave the closet open—this makes for one-motion storage and provides motivation to keep things neat.

The most important thing is what's important to *you*. Usually it's the hanging clothes. London sometimes creates a three-rod system if the closet has a high ceiling or the client isn't terribly tall. The top rod can be used for garment bags full of out-of-season clothes, so summer and winter apparel can be stored in the same closet. This is especially handy for urban lifestyles that include a lot of travel. Even in the middle of January, resort clothes are right there when you're ready to make your great escape.

Closet Accoutrements

Professional organizers unanimously recommend plastic hangers as opposed to wire, because they don't get tangled up as easily and they keep clothes looking nicer. These hangers are flexible and thick enough not to break and should always have a swivel head. Maxine Ordesky recommends installing a rod above shelf height for holding extra hangers. But she is quick to point out that the only extra hangers in the closet should

closets if they're small (36"), but adjacent larger closets have enough wall and door space to make this counterproductive. When there isn't a closet, she uses prefab wall units to create "a wall of closet space." These hold not only clothes and sweaters, but the TV, stereo, books, china—you name it!

Sliding or folding closet doors waste a lot of space, because you can't hang things on the backs of them. With sliding doors, you can

Courtesy Lillian Vernon Corp.

Left: **There are shoe bags that hang on hooks as well as over-the-door models, but whatever kind you choose, make sure it has enough pockets to hold all the shoes you wear regularly.**

be for clothes that are in the laundry, at the dry cleaners, or on your back!

Designed to hold belts, ties, and handbags, accessory holders function as specialized hangers that hang from the closet rod. There are also multiple-skirt hangers and slacks racks (which should always be open-ended or have swing-away arms for easy retrieval), blouse trees, and add-on suit hangers, all of which save space while keeping clothes organized. Hook clips attached to closet rods hold everything from umbrellas to ties and boots.

Ties, belts, scarves, and jewelry can also be stored in drawers outfitted with mini-compartments. Antique photographers' trays as well as sliding accessory trays work well for this.

There are many alternatives to the jumble of shoes usually found on the closet floor. Shoe racks are available in over-the-door models, metal floor racks, vinyl wall pouches, and cubbyhole shelves, as well as in tiered garment-type bags that

are suspended from the closet rod. You might also use existing shelves to store shoes, or install another shelf on top to use wasted space up high. (You can store seldom worn shoes in their boxes, but be sure to label them!)

To use wasted floor space, expert organizer Deniece Schofield suggests improvising a shoe rack with two tension rods. Place the first rod four inches from the back wall and about six inches from the floor; the other rod goes seven

inches from the back wall and two inches from the floor. The shoe heel catches over the back rod and the toe of the shoe rests on the front bar. Some commercial models are based on the same principle—metal dowels that expand from 20 to 36 inches. There are also various other shoe racks you can make yourself: pairs of ½" dowels offset in two 1 x 10s, which can go to the ceiling; angled brackets in adjustable track shelves.

There are hundreds of types

Left: Shelves can be put to good use in a closet for storing shoes, among other things.

of tie and belt racks. Ties can be stored on horizontal or swing-down ladders, on revolving tie and belt racks that attach to closet walls, or on telescoping or electric tie racks that fasten to the rod. These are battery operated and hold from thirty-five to fifty ties. If you have more than fifty ties, you'll have to use door or wall space. Simply install a row of hooks, or pegboard with S-hooks, to hang up ties, handbags, belts, scarves —even necklaces— in an unused corner of the closet.

While lightweight handbags can be hung up, this may put too much stress on the straps. Since leather needs to "breathe," store large purses on open shelves or in stacking baskets.

Garment bags now come in so many shapes and sizes for so many different uses that they should probably be re-dubbed "store-all bags." Once used simply for seldom-worn or out-of-season clothing, some bags feature shelves for storing hats, handbags, sweaters, scarves, and even

Hanging garment bags and on-the-floor sweater boxes can help organize your out-of-season wardrobe while keeping it safe from dust and moths.

Courtesy Lillian Vernon Corp.

hardware stores as well as by mail order. You can either buy the whole system or catch-as-catch-can with various components. If you plan to do it yourself, have a good idea of what you want, and shop around before you buy.

Larger cities also have consultants (professional organizers) who make their living cleaning out clients' closets and installing custom systems. Obviously, this is more expensive than doing it yourself, but the advantage is that with a consultant's experience and expertise you may end up with a more efficient closet setup. Pros can work miracles with small space and will design and build to meet your specific needs, even taking into account things such as how tall you are and whether you're right- or left-handed. A full-service designer will knock down walls, install cabinetry, lighting, and doors, paint the closet, and even put all your possessions back where they belong. Maxine Ordesky describes hiring a closet designer as the difference between buying two garments on sale as opposed to one beautiful dress you've always wanted.

Out-of-Season Clothes

Some apartment dwellers with extensive wardrobes use the dry cleaner's for off-season storage, but unless you're a purebred clotheshorse you should be able to find some wasted space around the house for dead storage of clothes. If you have an abun-

shoes. These can be a cheaper alternative to a complete closet system, but may not be as effective, over all. If you have limited closet space, the big boxy bags may take up more room than they're worth. Look to suit and dress bags for off-season storage, and check out shelves, drawers, and bins to organize your accessories.

There is a mind-boggling array of individual closet organizers and complete systems available in department and

Courtesy Williams-Sonoma/Hold Everything Catalogue

Storage can be improvised under a bed using a pull out box on wheels.

dance of closet space, simply allocate an out-of-the-way or extra closet, or a portion of the "active" closet, and use garment bags to store out-of-season clothes. These come in sizes for gowns, dresses, and suits, so even dead storage can be made more efficient by installing a double-rod system. And many bags come with sides or backing made of cedarwood to provide extra protection from moths.

But if closet space is at a premium, you'll have to find other places for dead storage of clothes. Under the bed is a classic spot, facilitated by built-in or roll-out drawers. Or you could simply put the clothes in your luggage—provided you travel only rarely—and slide the suitcases under the bed. Steamer trunks, wicker or cedar chests—any kind of large, boxy container with a lid—are multifunctional choices, as they can double as an end table in another room. A window seat will store clothes as well as blankets.

If you have a dry basement, you might install a double-rod system under the stairs and hang off-season clothes, in garment bags, down there. There are also many do-it-yourself storage closets you can build in the basement; or, simply use a couple of old wardrobes, outfitted with a double rod and shelves.

The Bed

Another traditional area of wasted space is under the bed. Many platform beds now feature deep drawers for storing blankets, linens, sweaters, or even shoes. You can also buy or build rolling storage drawers that fit under your existing bed. The same stacking-drawer system (manufactured by Kartell) used in the kitchen with a butcher-block top can be adapted to function as the base for your mattress—low banks of drawers arranged to form a platform.

Besides under the bed, there's the headboard, and possibly a footboard or bolster bins (with padded lids that run along the sides of the bed), which can be used for storage. Many ready-to-assemble platform beds feature book-cases as part of the head-board. Or, you can build your own bookcase—to the ceiling if you want—to fit over your existing bed.

Loft beds are probably the ultimate use of under-bed space. The area under the bed

Drawers built into the base of the bed are a more permanent solution to bedroom storage problems.

Right: **If you live in a high-ceilinged studio, a loft bed can double your living space by removing the bed from the main flow of traffic.**

can be used for desks, couches, closets, bookcases, box shelves, or dinettes; you could even have a loft desk over a regular bed. Loft beds are great for kids who share a room, since they guarantee privacy. It helps to have a high ceiling, but this isn't essential —if you just wanted closed storage underneath, the bed would only need to be four feet off the floor. Loft beds are usually custom-built; however, there are some knockdown units available.

Miscellaneous Bedroom Storage

Many closet systems feature drawers, so you may be able to eliminate your dresser. Some people use wall units, many designed to act as combination headboards and room dividers, as an alternative to dressers and chests of drawers. But if you do use a dresser, position it as close to the closet as possible. No matter where you keep your drawers, use drawer dividers

to separate your different categories of items.

Jewelry boxes are good for valuable pieces, but if you prefer open storage of earrings, for instance, use T-headed pins on a pretty pillow or a cloth-covered board. Hang large jewelry—African necklaces, strings of beads, metal belts—from pegs on the wall or in the closet.

Keep blankets in a chest or a window seat, or in under-the-bed drawers. Deniece Schofield suggests you also store linens in the bedroom, where they help minimize the chore of changing the bed.

Nightstands are notorious space-wasters, often functioning only to support the bedside reading lamp and to collect clutter. They should at least have some drawers in order to earn their keep. If you usually go directly to the bedroom to change clothes when you get home, a nightstand drawer might be a good place to put what Maxine Ordesky calls your "staging area." This is where you keep your keys, extra eyeglasses, letters to be mailed, pocket change—everything you're bringing in or taking out. Depending on your lifestyle, this area might be in the kitchen, den, or office—it should be wherever you go first. It doesn't have to be neat, but it should be easily accessible.

Kids' Rooms

Babies' rooms are often overrun with diapers, stuffed animals, clothes still too big, and clothes already too small. Children's rooms may look like a hurricane just swept through, with toys, clothes, and books tossed every which way, without regard for life or limb.

Toy boxes are the traditional way to organize an overflow of toys, but they make it hard to retrieve old favorites. An alternative is track-and-bracket shelves installed at the child's level, which can be adjusted as he or she grows. Toys can be stored by category in la-

Below: **This pocketed toy holder will hold everything from shoes to toothbrushes, and has a fanciful design kids love. If you get kids involved in choosing their own storage organizers, they'll be more likely to use them.**

Judd Pilossof

belled dishpans or stacking bins: small cars, Tinker Toys, blocks, Legos, dolls, crayons, etc. This makes it easy for children to clean up their messes —they can just toss the stuff in the appropriate container— and helps them learn organization to boot.

Some toys can be hung on pegboard; you could even paint on the outlines of toys so it's clear what goes where. Another idea is to buy a spring-loaded pole and attach

S-hooks to it, then hang stuffed animals using café curtain hooks. Or you might hang a small hammock in the corner of the room for holding dolls and stuffed animals. Baskets are also good for storing stuffed animals.

There are slide-in racks for puzzles which keep them intact and also separate them from one another for easy retrieval. A bank of cubbyholes will hold school and art supplies. In some rough-and-

tumble rooms, bicycles can be hung from the ceiling or the wall and function as part of the décor.

If you prefer closed storage for toys, consider buying some mini-lockers (the kind you used in phys. ed.) and painting them bright, fun colors. Lockers allow children to keep toys in separate compartments, but be sure the kids are old enough not to smash their fingers in the metal doors.

A bulletin board or corkboard is a must for hanging artwork and posters; that way you'll save the wall from tape marks and thumbtack holes. Some children's rooms boast an entire wall of corkboard. Schofield suggests you store

Courtesy Heller

Stacking baskets are colorful, durable, and great for getting kids to clean up their own clutter—all they need to do is toss toys in the appropriate bin.

Those old standbys, concrete blocks and boards, are an inexpensive way to get a child's things organized fast.

large posters or artwork from school flat, in an artist's portfolio; or roll them up and put them in the long tubes that wrapping paper comes in. Label the tubes and stick them in a tall bin or basket.

Many bunk beds now feature built-in storage. Some traditional "one on top of another" units offer attached shelves and fold-down desks; others are positioned at right angles, with a study area tucked in next to the lower bunk. For a child who has the luxury of his or her own room, an elevated bed with building-block style drawers beneath it offers quite a bit of added storage space.

Kids' closets can be organized with scaled-down systems just like the one in your room; the only difference is that rods and shelves should be adjustable, so they can grow with the child. Just as you did with your closet, take the child's needs and priorities into account. Does he need space for sports equipment?

rooms—one for outgrown clothes you want to save, another for clothes they've yet to grow into.

When planning storage in your children's rooms, talk to them about it. Explain the options you're considering and ask how they'd most like things to be. After all, they're the ones who'll be using it and held responsible for keeping it neat, and often they'll come up with some innovative ideas of their own.

When children share a room, it's important to provide each with a personal storage space. Plan kids' rooms for all activities, including fun. A fireman's pole makes getting up in the morning an adventure, and is also appreciated on rainy afternoons.

E. Allen McGee/FPG International

Will her wardrobe be expanding as years go by?

Stacking bins work well for underwear, socks, shirts, and scarves; hooks are great for coats and hats. Deniece Schofield recommends keeping shoes in a shallow dishpan—that way kids can toss them in easily and they'll be out of the way. (Even though the shoes are slightly jumbled, they are penned up in one place.) For kids who are growing rapidly, Deniece suggests keeping two cardboard cartons in their

A STEP-BY-STEP GUIDE
PROJECT 4
Window Storage Seat

Only you know how large a storage seat you can afford to make. Take these three preliminary measurements: height, depth (front to back), and length (end to end).

For the front and back, cut two pieces of ¾" plywood to the "length" measurement by 2" less than the height you need. To serve as reinforcement, cut two pieces of 2 x 2, 4½" less than your "length," and four pieces of 2 x 2, 2" less than the height. Countersink, screw (use 2¼" flat-topped wood screws), and glue the 2 x 2s to the front and back. Sand the outside edges to a smooth, rounded shape.

Cut the two sides from ¾" plywood to 2" less than the "height" you need, by 1½" less than your "depth" measurement. Stand the front and back up; countersink, screw, and glue the sides to the front and back.

Cut a piece of ¾" plywood for the bottom; notch the corners to accommodate the 2 x 2 interior supports. Glue and nail it into place.

You could use hinges for the top, but if you want to keep it simple, try a peg and guide lift-off top. First cut a plywood top that will overlap all edges by approximately ¼". Sand all four edges to a smooth, rounded shape. Drill a ⅜" diameter hole into each of the

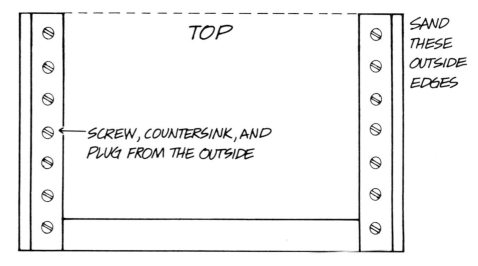

COUNTER SINK, SCREW, AND GLUE THE 2"X2" TO THE FRONT AND BACK LIKE THIS:

TOP

SCREW, COUNTERSINK, AND PLUG FROM THE OUTSIDE

SAND THESE OUTSIDE EDGES

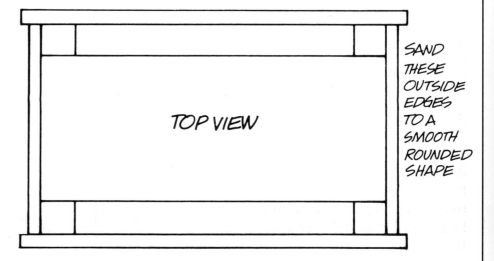

STAND THE FRONT AND BACK UP AND COUNTERSINK, SCREW, AND GLUE THE SIDES TO THE FRONT AND BACK AS SUCH;

TOP VIEW

SAND THESE OUTSIDE EDGES TO A SMOOTH ROUNDED SHAPE

SIDE VIEW

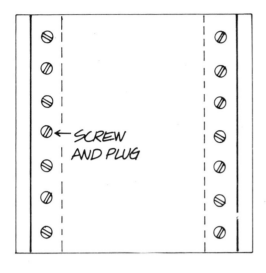

← SCREW AND PLUG

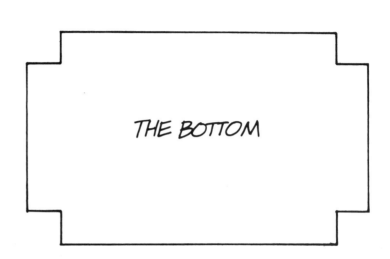

THE BOTTOM

four corner 2 x 2s. Glue a ⅜" dowel into each hole, leaving a little less than ½" exposed. Round the exposed ends (a pencil sharpener works well if you do it before gluing the pegs in). Carefully drill ½" guide holes into the appropriate spots on the underside of the top.

Although the sides of the top overlap, so you technically don't need handles, traditional furniture of this type may have finger- and thumbholes on either side, or rope handles.

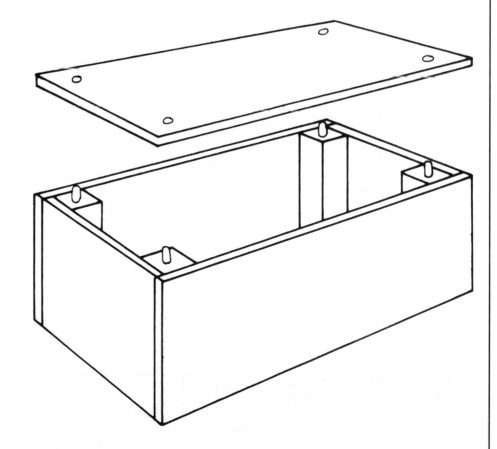

IN ONE SECTION YOU MAY WANT TO PUT A SMALL PULL OUT SHELF

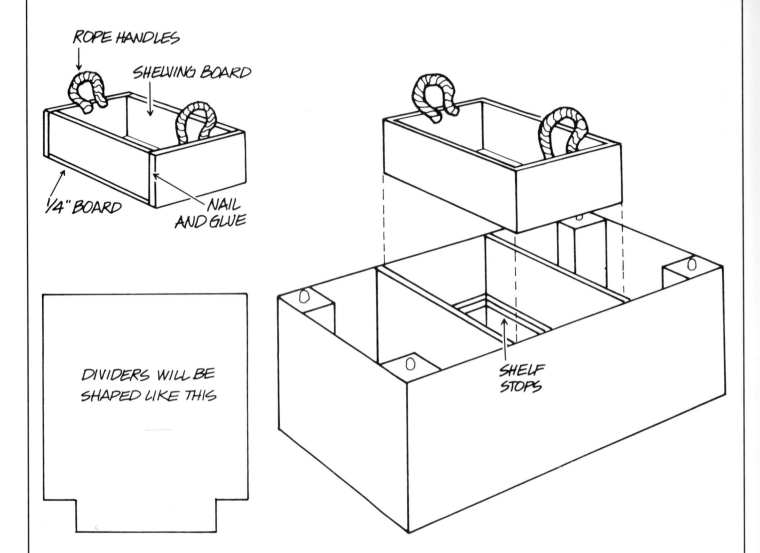

ROPE HANDLES

SHELVING BOARD

¼" BOARD

NAIL AND GLUE

DIVIDERS WILL BE SHAPED LIKE THIS

SHELF STOPS

You may want to add dividers on the inside, to help keep stuff separate. Cut plywood to fit beneath the top 2 x 2 support; remember to notch the bottom to accommodate bottom 2 x 2s. Space these dividers no less than two feet apart; countersink 2" finishing nails and fill holes with putty.

In one section, you might want to add a small pull-out shelf (see illustration).

Finish both sides of every exposed board, inside and out.

*If you need a heavy-duty storage seat, substitute 3½" carriage bolts for the screw-and-plug construction.

*For decoration and ventilation, you may want to cut holes in the sides in the shapes of hearts, flowers, ducks, sheep, pigs, etc.

*Cedar veneer might be a great investment for wool-lovers. Just glue and tack it to the interior.

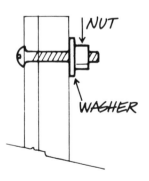

CARRIAGE BOLT

NUT

WASHER

Home Office

Most homes include a desk or area where bills are paid, letters written, shopping lists made out, and important papers stored. Often this is in a corner of the kitchen or bedroom, but the ''home office'' can also be found in the living room, dining room, or family room. Or it may even be a room unto itself.

A lot depends on the kind of work you do in this space. If it's just used once a month to pay bills, it may be nothing more than a drawer in the kitchen equipped with pencil, paper, stamps, and paper clips. But if you operate a sideline business or full-time freelance career from your home, your office must be in a separate room and used exclusively as an office in order for the I.R.S. to allow it as a deduction. Also, if you have a family or share the house with other people, it's much easier to avoid distractions if you work in a room with a door that can be closed.

If you want to add an office to your small home or apartment, you need to decide whether to make it mainly living or work space—you can opt for a convertible bed or a fold-out desk, for instance. Some studio-apartment dwellers have desks that are suspended from the ceiling and lowered with pulleys. In older homes, a large closet might be converted to a mini-office, or a semiprivate office can be created in a corner of a room by suspending a large piece of plywood or a door between two to-the-ceiling bookcases.

So as usual, you need to plan work and storage space to meet *your* needs—an artist or photographer will have different requirements than a writer or independent sales rep. If you receive clients in the office, it should look businesslike as well as being comfortable to work in. Otherwise,

A mini-office can be nestled in a corner of your guest room or bedroom. If possible, place the desk so you can see out a window, because after a lot of reading or close work, it helps to rest your eyes on something far away.

the office can be as casual or as formal as you want as long as it's efficient.

But wherever your office is, and no matter how you use it, store everything you need in the vicinity. Nothing is more frustrating than having to trek to another room every time you need to sharpen your pencil or answer the phone. Create a convenient place for storing scissors, tape, envelopes, rulers, notepads—everything you use regularly.

Office Equipment

Conventional desks—the flat-topped, knee-hole type found in most offices—usually have file drawers that may eliminate the need for a filing cabinet. These desks have large work surfaces and average about thirty inches tall; new ones are expensive (especially those made of wood), but you may be able to find a good used model at half the normal price.

My desk is simply a hardwood door supported by a filing cabinet at one end and a

Left: A small antique desk makes a charming addition to a living room. It also affords the luxury of paying bills and writing letters in a pleasant, comfortable atmosphere.

Strictly-business office equipment may be your best bet if you work full-time as a freelancer, or are serious about building a home business. Its no-nonsense look encourages you to get right to work.

Courtesy Techline/By Marshall Erdman and Associates, Inc.

bookcase at the other; a filing cabinet at either end works just as well. And any top will do as long as it's wide enough to work on (at least 18–24"), and thick enough to afford a solid working surface. You could paint it with a mat paint (glossy finish reflects light and makes it harder to see what you're doing), stain it, or even laminate it.

Some desks feature a typing carriage; others have a slide-out shelf for the typewriter. Or an old-fashioned wheeled typing table can be positioned adjacent to the desk and rolled into a closet for storage. A typewriter can be stored in its case on a shelf, in a cupboard, or on a pull-out shelf in a cabinet behind the desk.

Desktop organizers fit over the top of the desk and provide storage for things like phone books, stationery and envelopes, reference books, memo pads, audiotapes, manuals, catalogues, etc. These are designed to not take up valuable desk space—the area under the shelf or shelves is left open for the phone, calculator, and supplies.

Filing cabinets are the tried-and-true way to store all kinds of papers and correspondence. They come in both two-drawer and four-drawer models, made of metal or wood. (You'll also find cardboard cabinets but these aren't recommended.) Vertical files extend into the room and

Left: **Professional office equipment is engineered for efficiency. Every good chair has a pneumatic height that adjusts to suit each occupant.**

Courtesy Spelman

When not employed as a desk, this rolling table serves as a buffet at parties.

performs better under heavy loads; when you pull out the drawer the suspension system slides out with it, providing support. With non-suspension systems, the drawers slide on ball bearings or tiny wheels; these have a tendency to tip over when you pull out a heavily laden drawer.

Pendaflex suspension file folders hang from a metal rack inside the drawer, which is much easier to use than files that are simply stacked into a drawer. The customary way is to file things alphabetically, but use whatever system works for you.

If you don't have enough papers to merit a filing cabinet, there are cardboard-box files and accordion files that will help you keep organized. A metal strongbox provides extra protection for important papers. Or consider investing in a roll-away file. The top opens to reveal your files, so there's no need for an expensive suspension system, and you have the protection of steel. Some-

the drawers' contents are viewed from front to back when opened; lateral files require more wall space but the entire contents of a drawer are visible when they're opened just a few inches. Metal is flame-resistant and thus more secure for storing valuable documents such as birth certificates, wills, deeds, etc.

The quality—and price—of a filing cabinet is determined by the track system for the drawers. A full-suspension roller system is best because it what more expensive roll-away models feature a second drawer below the first—usually just a shelf.

Bookshelves are good for books, obviously, but they can also be used for projects in progress; for instance, as an editor I use shelves under my desk for manuscripts. You can have an entire wall of book-cases, or one behind or beside your desk for easy access. Shelves should be at least 9" wide for standard books, 12" wide for larger books or magazines. Or, if your paperback collection has overpowered the bookcase, consider purchasing some wire book racks, which can be mounted on a door or wall.

For additional office storage, credenzas are good as a holding area for ongoing projects that you want to keep out of sight. (Just be sure to keep everything neatly stacked and categorized.) Also, modular stacking drawer units can be put together into a complete storage wall. Rolling carts are good for large ongoing projects, while plastic desk trays or shallow wire baskets arranged on a shelf or desktop work well for keeping small projects separate.

A large wastebasket is a must for "storing" papers to be discarded; place it under or near your desk for disposal of junk mail and old notes.

Organize your desk using the point-of-first-use principle—keep everything you use often within easy reach. Keep pens and pencils either in a top drawer or, even better, in

Books take up a lot of room once you start collecting them. This office uses otherwise wasted wall space by taking bookcases all the way to the ceiling. The sliding library ladder makes retrieving out-of-reach books a snap.

a mug or small ceramic container on top of your desk. Keep paper in a drawer or a tiered desk organizer, and store surplus in a cupboard or closet. Paper clips belong in a divided desk drawer or in a caddy on the desktop. Personally, I prefer open storage for clips as well as correction fluid, Post-its, a stapler—everything I use on a daily basis.

Stephanie Culp suggests organizing your incoming papers into four categories: "to do," "to pay," "to file," and "to read." Use stacking wire baskets for "to do" and "to pay" so you can see what's in there—"to do" belongs on top, "to pay" on the bottom. She suggests you keep your stuff to be filed in a roomy wicker basket under the desk. Things to be read also belong in a wicker basket, but it should have a handle so you can carry it from room to room when you're ready to catch up on your reading.

A Rolodex is better for storing names and numbers than an address book because it's easily kept up-to-date by simply removing and replacing the pages. You can also insert business cards and write little notes about clients or friends —birthdays, anniversaries, temporary addresses—on the backs of cards.

Your phone should be near the desk, and an answering machine is helpful for avoiding interruptions when you're working, as well as to keep track of important calls when you're out.

If you own a computer, you already know how good it is at storing vast quantities of information. You may also know about the vast array of computer furniture—mobile terminal tables, printer stands, and work stations; fold-out monitor platforms that free up desk space; computer cabinets that can be closed when not in use; pull-out keyboard shelves and sectioned above-desk shelves with adjustable dividers to keep software and manuals within easy reach. If your computer stand is separate from your desk, your most important piece of office furniture is probably a rolling adjustable chair, so you can switch from one to the other painlessly.

Hobby Rooms

If you have a separate room set aside for sewing, woodworking, or some other craft, be grateful—those of us who must make living space do double duty think you've got the best of all possible worlds. But anything is possible—I used to think I had to have a basement in order to batik, because it's so messy (hot wax and dyes), plus that's where I'd always done it. But apartment living forced me to adapt. Now my batik supplies are kept in vegetable crates on a shelf in the hall closet, and I bring them to the dining area when I'm ready to work. (I cover the table with a plastic

Computer stations typically provide space for storing books and paper as well as for the terminal, keyboard, and printer.

tarp first.) Dyeing takes place in five-gallon buckets in the bathtub.

But whether you have a bona-fide workshop or must make do with a corner of some other room, how you store your materials depends on what they happen to be. Potters need plastic or metal garbage cans to keep clay moist, for instance; photographers need a dustproof place to store negatives, and a file for prints. (Accordion files with alphabetical pockets and a master list of what's found in each pocket work well for prints; slides can be stored in vinyl sheets in a loose-leaf binder, or in small boxes, numbered against a master list.) Darkroom chemicals and supplies are best stored on open shelves for instant retrieval.

For visual artists, taborets and stack trays are good for keeping materials organized, while magnetic bars can be used to hang up brushes, T-

If your hobby is gardening and raising houseplants, you may be able to get by with using the kitchen table for those occasional activities which require space indoors. Potting soil, containers, and a trowel could be stored in a nearby cupboard or under the sink.

Courtesy Quaker Maid

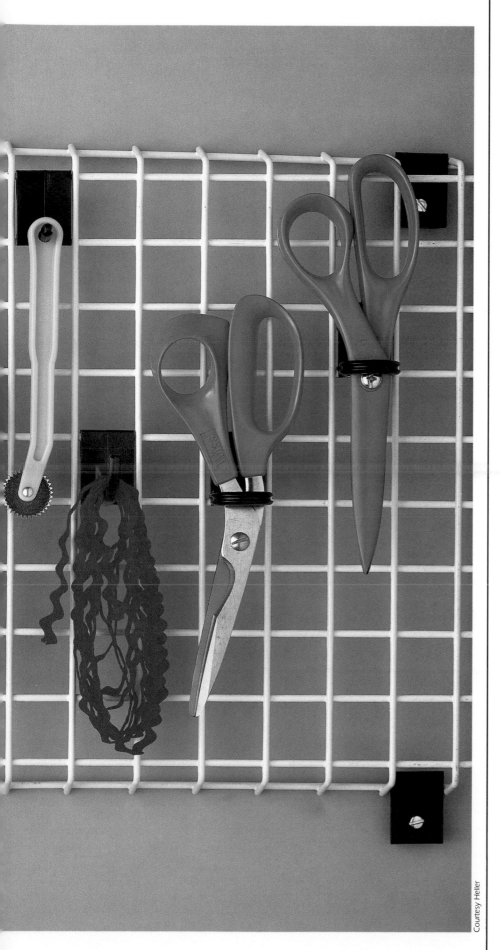

A simple grid that organizes sewing supplies can be like the proverbial "stitch in time that saves nine." Since everything you need is visible and within easy reach, you'll eliminate a lot of wasted motion.

squares, and knives. Rotary organizers or desk caddies hold pens, pencils, brushes, small knives, etc. Steel flat files serve as "filing cabinets" for finished work as well as for paper and art board. Another option for drawings or plans are steel roll files, where the work is rolled up and stashed in its own cubby. Stretched canvases are usually stored in vertical slots. These are easier to clean if the dividers are removable.

For home workshops, pegboard is the old standby for hanging tools, but ceramic magnet bars also work well. And steel outline systems, designed to hang up large tools like shovels and rakes, can be adapted for the shop. Rotating tool caddies hold small tools such as screwdrivers, pliers, and files.

Knitters might choose to store yarn in open baskets for a colorful decorative accent; a jeweler could keep small treasures—beads, fasteners, stones, silver wire—in storage cabinets with see-through

Courtesy Heller

plastic drawers. Collections of various sorts can be contained in tackle or tool boxes, though any attractive collection— rocks, shells, scarves, dolls, coins, etc.—deserves to be displayed.

Open shelves above the work area function for lots of materials: a weaver's large spools of thread, baby-food jars full of buttons or other small notions, Magic Markers in stand-up caddies, stacking bins full of small shop items

like electric connectors, solder, and crowfoot wrenches. And not just shop tools can be hung on the wall. Some seamstresses use pegboard to hang scissors, tape measures, and spools of thread.

You get the idea. Tailor your storage solutions to your own particular needs. But no matter what your hobby, remember the point-of-first-use principle and keep anything you use often in an easily accessible spot. Store less often used material in cupboards, but keep them organized with some of the same products you've used elsewhere in the house. Use dishpans, bins, or baskets to keep large stuff separate. Smaller items can be sorted into ice-cube trays, plastic bags—even pillboxes.

If price is no object and you've got the space, a wall unit adapts nicely to become a "hobby unit." If space is limited, incorporate storage under tables, workbench, or counters. Metal, under-shelf drawers work well for tools, tubes of paint, sewing notions, whatever. These shelves can also be bolted under a table or bench. The tops of baby-food jars can be nailed to the underside of a shelf so

Christopher Bain

Left: **A toolbox can be used to organize much more than just tools—photography or art supplies, even makeup.**

the jars (full of nuts and bolts or hooks and eyes, take your pick) hang right in front of you. A commercial version based on this principle features a rotating rack of twelve jars that's mounted to the wall or workbench.

Consider buying or building a wall-storage cabinet or converting a closet to a workshop with a fold-down work area when space is extremely tight. Wall-storage cabinets such as Black and Decker's Workmate or the Shopkeep from Arrow Group Industries are great for organizing tools in a small space. They feature things like a tilt-out tool tray; a folding worktable/vise unit; pegboard for hanging tools; plastic drawers for storing screws, bolts, nails, etc.; racks for brochures and owner's manuals; and a tote tray for carrying tools to jobs around the house. And they can be locked to keep kids from playing with dangerous tools.

A picnic basket is a decorative way to store knitting supplies.

Christopher Bain

A STEP-BY-STEP GUIDE

PROJECT 5
Removable Hobby Closet/Work Station

This project does not require putting nails in your closet walls, so you can build it even if you rent; screws are used as fasteners, so it's a simple matter to take it apart when you move. Once the basic frame is in place, you can add a drafting table, computer desk, hobby corner—whatever your heart desires. The design allows you to leave the door on the closet so you can hide work, or you could remove the door and use this space for decorative purposes—craft projects, knickknacks, or heirlooms might be displayed. A friend's grandmother raised African violets under a grow light in her closet.

To begin, take some preliminary measurements: from the floor to approximately one foot from the ceiling (this will be your "height" and will allow you to put a deep shelf above your work area); "depth," from the inside wall to the back wall; "width," from side wall to side wall inside the closet.

To construct the sides of the frame, cut four 2 x 4s to a length 1" less than your "height" measurement. Cut squares in the ends of the 2 x 4s to accommodate 2 x 2s (measure the 2 x 2s to see exactly how big to make these notches). Then measure the "short side" of your 2 x 4s; cut

MEASURE THE WIDTH OF YOUR 2"x2" (S).
CUT SQUARES IN THE ENDS OF THE FOUR (4)
2"x4" (S) TO THAT MEASUREMENT, AS SUCH;

MEASURE THE "SHORT SIDE" OF YOUR 2"x4"(S).
CUT TWO (2) 2"x2" TO THAT MEASUREMENT.
NAIL OR SCREW THEM ONTO TWO OF THE 2"x4"(S)
AS SUCH;

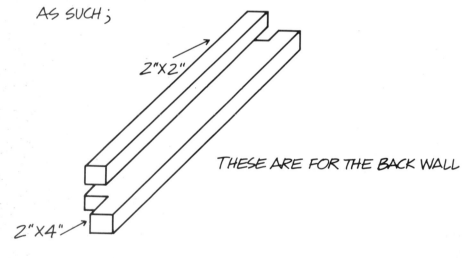

2"x2"

THESE ARE FOR THE BACK WALL

2"x4"

TO MAKE HOME-MADE CORNER BRACES,
CUT A 2"x4" AS SUCH;

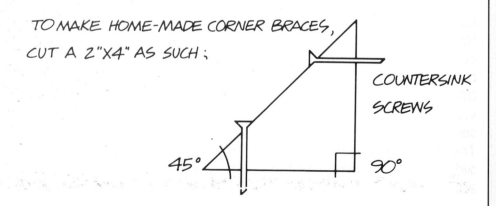

COUNTERSINK
SCREWS

45°   90°

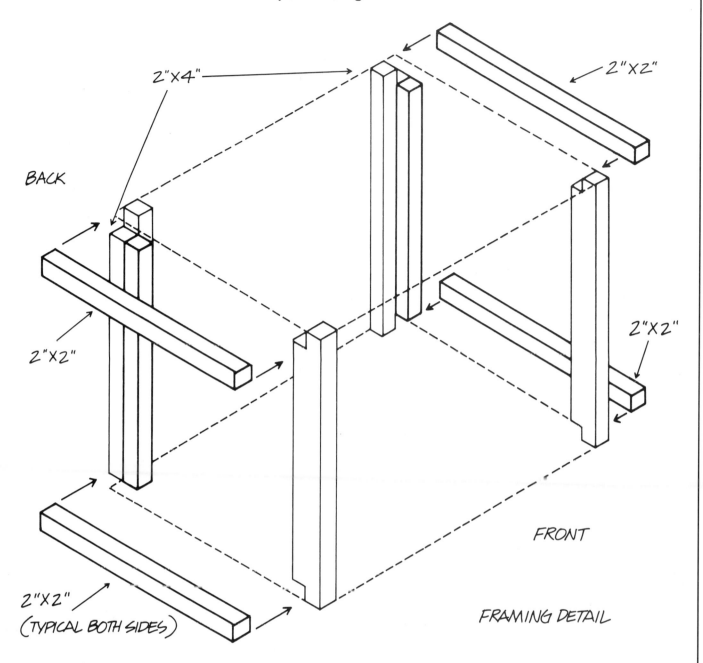

BACK

2"x4"

2"x2"

2"x2"

2"x2"

2"x2"
(TYPICAL BOTH SIDES)

FRONT

FRAMING DETAIL

two 2 x 2s to that measurement. Screw them onto two of the 2 x 4s. These are for the back wall.

Stand one 2 x 4 in the front corner of the closet, broad side toward the side wall, with the cut-out section toward the back. Stand one 2 x 4 in the back corner, broad side toward the back wall, cut out section toward the corner. The 2 x 2 pieces should then slide into place along the top and bottom.

Secure the four corners using commercially available corner braces, or homemade corner braces. To make corner braces, cut a 2 x 4 into a wedge. Repeat above steps for opposite wall.

For the back, cut a piece of pegboard, particle board, or ¼" plywood that will cover the area between the 2 x 2s on either side—½" above the top of the frame and to the floor (or at least below the desktop). If you have a wide

closet, or are planning on supporting a lot of weight on the shelves, tack 2 x 2s on the back of your backboard for extra strength. These reinforcing 2 x 2s should be placed approximately 12" to 18" apart. Screw or nail the back to the exposed 2 x 4s of the frame.

For your top shelf, purchase 1" pine shelving in the width you desire. If you have a table saw, you can rip (cut lengthwise) a piece and fit the top

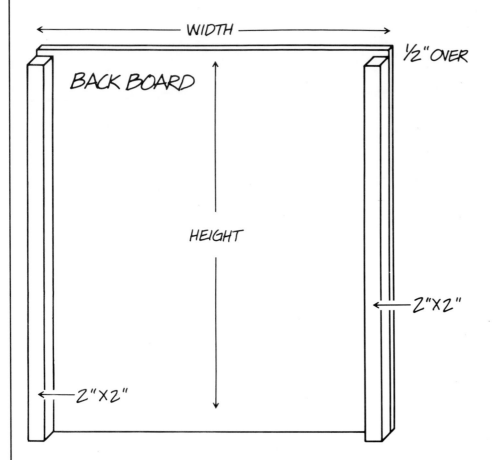

WIDTH

BACK BOARD

½" OVER

HEIGHT

2"×2"

2"×2"

shelf perfectly in your closet; if not, you can come close using the various widths available. Cut the shelving slightly smaller than the "width" of the closet and screw or nail it onto the top 2 x 2s of the sides. Be sure the back piece of shelving butts up against the back, which helps to brace it.

This completes the basic frame. From here on you'll want to tailor the work closet to your specific needs. Detailed measurement and planning will depend on the exact size of your closet and on what features you wish to build in.

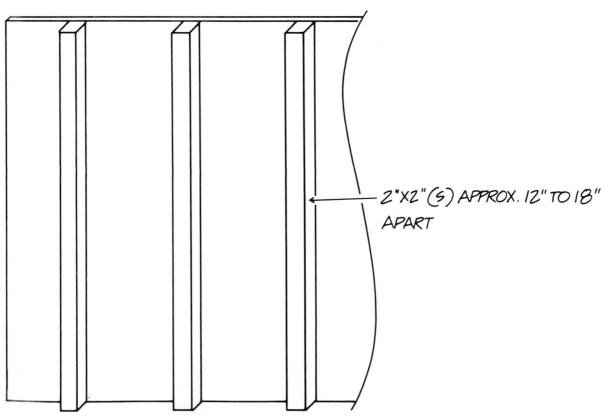

BACK VIEW OF BACK

2"×2"(S) APPROX. 12" TO 18" APART

REMEMBER, THE PIECES IN THE BACK AND FRONT
WILL HAVE TO BE CUT TO ACCOMODATE THE
SIDE SUPPORTS, LIKE THIS;

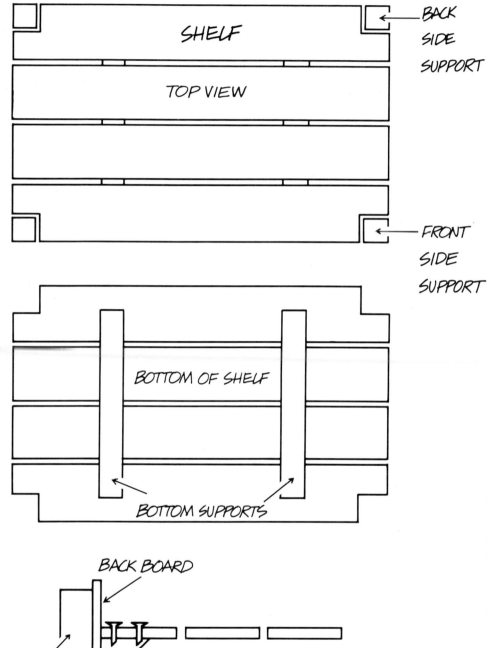

SHELF

TOP VIEW

BACK
SIDE
SUPPORT

FRONT
SIDE
SUPPORT

BOTTOM OF SHELF

BOTTOM SUPPORTS

BACK BOARD

2"X2"

CORNER BRACES

SIDE VIEW

SHELVES: For each shelf, cut two side supports from 1 x 2, 1 x 3, or scrap. Screw or nail these to the side section at the height you want your shelf to rest. Cut your shelving to a length just a little less than the "width" of your closet. Remember, the pieces in back and front will have to be cut to accommodate the side supports (see illustration).

If you added extra support to the back (2 x 2s), brace your shelves with corner braces, using the 2 x 2s as studs. If your shelf is more than one board wide, attach them by nailing and gluing or screwing and gluing a 1 x 2, 1 x 3, or scrap across their bottoms for extra support.

DRAFTING TABLE

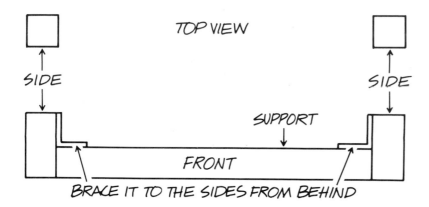

TOP VIEW

SIDE — SIDE

SUPPORT

FRONT

BRACE IT TO THE SIDES FROM BEHIND

YOUR DRAFTING TABLE BOARD SHOULD BE ABOUT 1" SHORTER THAN THE PRESENT DEPTH OF YOUR CLOSET. AT THE TOP, SECURE A 2"X4" ACCROSS THE BACK WALL. AT THE BOTTOM, NAIL AND GLUE ANOTHER 1"X1" STRIP, AS SUCH:

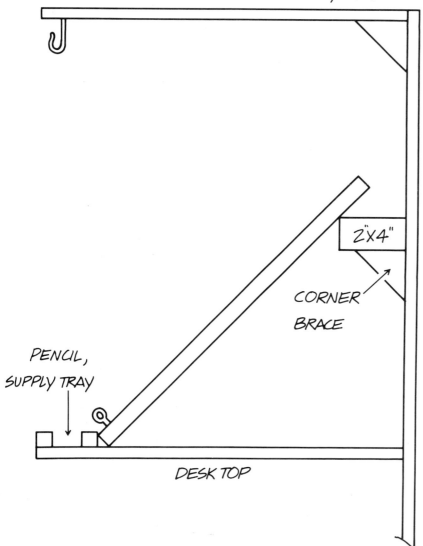

2"X4"

CORNER BRACE

PENCIL, SUPPLY TRAY

DESK TOP

If you plan to use this area for an electric typewriter or as a computer work station, cut cable and power-cord holes in the back of your shelves and desktop before installing.

DESKTOP, WORK AREA: Build your desktop or work area in the same way you constructed the shelves. Substitute quality ¾" plywood for the shelving for a smooth, even surface. For support, in addition to the corner braces, cut a 2 x 4 to fit between the two sides, for the desktop to rest upon.

DRAFTING TABLE: In order to use the area under the drafting table, first build a desktop to the depth of the closet, at the level you choose for the bottom of your table. Nail and glue a 1" x 1" strip across the top of the front of this shelf; add another 1 x 1 strip about 2" behind it. This will serve as a pencil tray; the inside 1 x 1 will help hold the drafting board upright.

Your drafting board should be about 1" shorter than the present depth of your closet. At the top, secure a 2 x 4 across the back wall; use corner braces. The drafting table will lean up against this shelf. You can place rope loops on the sides of your drafting board, hooks on an upper shelf, and lift and hang the drafting table to get to the space below. It can be used as a flat desktop or organized and divided with 1 x 1s to store supplies.

COMPUTER WORK STA-TION: Cut plenty of wide cable channels in the back of your desktop and shelves and 1" x 9" slot to feed paper to the printer. Be sure the shelf for the printer is nailed or screwed and glued securely to minimize vibration and racket. If you are feeding and recovering the paper through slots on the shelf, you might want to build a door to enclose the printer. (A slot can be cut in the front of the shelf to feed printed paper down into a tray on the work area.) A corkboard on the back wall is great for holding notes and materials. Use a soft light to minimize glare.

POWER: You'll probably need more than one plug in your work/hobby area. Multi-socketed power strips with circuit breakers are available in many stores; they come with mounting brackets and can be placed wherever most convenient.

HOBBY CORNER: A pegboard back wall is good for this design. To hold pencils, carving tools, screwdrivers, etc., drill ½" holes into the small side of a 2 x 4 and mount them across the sides and back of your work area. Jar lids can be tacked to the bottom of the shelf above your work space; the jars can be filled with tacks, screws, zippers, beads, etc.—whatever you need for your hobby. If you use a lot of electricity in your craft, you may want to mount a power strip on your desktop.

COMPUTER DESK

WIDE SLOTS FOR CABLE HEADS AND POWER CORDS

SLOT FOR PRINTER PAPER

SLOT IN FRONT OF SHELF TO DROP PRINTOUT TO A TRAY ON DESK TOP.

PAPER SOURCE

Bathrooms

Designer bathrooms may have everything from Jacuzzis and Nautilus machines to TVs and phones; some even include sitting rooms, libraries, and wet bars. Architectural features such as floor-to-ceiling mirrors, picture windows, and fireplaces are commonplace, as are decorator touches—vases of flowers, artwork and sculpture, houseplants. This may seem a trifle decadent, but in fact the bathroom is the most used room in the house after the kitchen, so it makes sense to create a pleasing environment. And even if your bathroom is of the bare-bones-functional variety, you can gussy it up with convenient and attractive storage.

First of all, scout out wasted space—on walls, above the toilet or tub, at the end of a vanity, under the sink or toilet tank—and look for ways to take advantage of it. Add cabinets above the sink, triangular shelves or cupboards in cor-

Right: Shelves can be used throughout the bathroom for storing everything from towels to toiletries and cosmetics. If you have space, a small table or chest of drawers will also help keep clutter under control.

Below: The tambour cabinets in this bathroom provide closed storage for supplies while repeating the design of the paneling.

Many manufacturers now offer fine cabinetry for the bathroom as well as for the kitchen. Most lines feature a variety of components, which allow you to personalize your bathroom storage system.

ners, extra hooks for towels, robes, and clothes. Attach over-the-door towel racks and shelves to the inside of the door. Pull-out drawers and bins available in plastic, wire, vinyl-coated wire, or wood can be installed in a vanity base cabinet on standard drawer slides or using their own special hardware. The space between the sink and the medicine cabinet can be converted to a fold-down drawer, or even just open shelves. The empty space above the tub can be used for shelves or narrow cabinets.

Consider racks, pull-out bins, stair-step shelves, and lazy Susans for storing things out of sight. Also think about what you want to display.

For instance, towels are usually bright and colorful, so consider giving them open storage. Clean towels can be neatly rolled and stashed in a handwoven basket or lacquered bin, stacked on open shelves above the toilet or on high shelves above the back

of the tub, even rolled up and placed in a wine rack painted to match the décor. That way you can use the linen closet space that was devoted to towels for less attractive items or a backup supply of shampoo, soap, toilet paper, etc.

For towels in use, consider towel ladders that run from floor to ceiling, tension poles with outstretched bars at varying heights, a wall grid, a standing towel rack, or even a hat rack; pegs are also handy. A garden trellis can be adapted to the bath for hanging towels and house plants—sand and stain it, add hooks, and attach to wall studs. If you simply want to add more towel rods to the wall, place them at least 26" above or below existing rods to allow for drying towels. (Towel rings are okay for hanging dry towels, but aren't really adequate for wet ones.)

If your medicine chest is overflowing with everything from aspirin to cosmetics, consider installing another one on the opposite or an adjacent wall (at a 90 degree angle) to handle the excess; that way you can also see the back of your head without resorting to a hand mirror. Or simply install another cabinet beside the first, above the sink. Yet another option is to build a between-the-studs recessed cabinet. But your first step should be to sort through all the makeup and medicine and get rid of anything that's expired or that you don't use— you may have enough room without adding a cabinet.

Courtesy Quaker Maid

Like most other rooms, the bathroom often has a lot of underdeveloped wall space. Look for ways to make the most of it.

Or maybe you like to catch up on your reading in the privacy of the loo, so there's a perpetual pile of magazines getting water-spotted and warped beside the tub. A between-the-studs magazine rack may be just what's needed, or simply install bookshelves over the toilet.

Bamboo and wicker shelves designed for storing cosmetics and toiletries work well above the toilet, as do wall brackets with clear glass shelves. There are freestanding closed stor-

age modules that sit on top of the tank, as well as specially made tension poles that support shelves from tank to ceiling. Just remember that you may need to take the lid off the tank from time to time, so allow enough room to do so. (This is the drawback of free-standing tank-top modules—in case of emergency they have to be lifted off, making you lose valuable seconds as the toilet overflows.)

Creative organizer Maxine Ordesky designs custom drawer dividers for her clients to use in storing makeup and jewelry. Made of Lucite, they lift out for easy cleaning. You can improvise a similar setup using flatware trays or snap-together drawer dividers—one section for lipsticks, another for eye shadow and mascara, etc. Or adapt a compartmentalized desk caddy for cosmetics storage. Display a bouquet

A shower caddy that fits in a corner is an ingenious way to clear up the clutter that usually lines the edge of the tub.

of cosmetics brushes in a small basket, vase, brandy snifter, jar, or crock.

Organizational expert Deniece Schofield suggests hanging baskets on the wall—one for each family member—to hold bathroom cups, toothbrushes, toothpaste, hand towels, and washrags (over the edge). She also suggests you store children's bath toys in a mesh bag and hang it above the tub when not in use. Or simply store the toys in a plastic basket that can be left in the tub as the water drains out; it's a simple matter for adults to lift out the basket when they're ready to bathe.

Shower caddies can be hung from the shower head—these supply a rack for soap, loofah, shampoo, razor, washrag, etc., and are usually made of wire or feature slanted shelves to prevent water from pooling under shampoo bottles. There are also bath "towers," snap-locking, self-draining, plastic shelves with chrome bars to hold washrags, scrub brushes, etc., that fit into the corner of the tub or shower by means of a tension rod. For tubs, an over-the-tub rack will hold magazines, soap, toys, shampoo, etc. A more artsy approach is to use a ceramic saucer or plate to hold soap, loofah, body sponges, bath oil, etc. Or use a large seashell or a rock with crevices as a soap holder.

If you have an old-fashioned sink on legs or a wall-hung model and no vanity, add a gathered skirt in a fabric that matches the décor so you can use this area for closed storage. Velcro can be sewn on to the inside of the skirt and attached to the sink with a hot-glue gun so the fabric comes off easily for laundering. Store cleaning supplies (in wire or plastic baskets), bins of bathroom supplies, towels, or dirty laundry under the sink and out of sight. You can even add shelves for additional storage.

If you're low on counter space but have space in the room, use a small table to store toiletries and personal grooming supplies—a sort of makeshift dressing table. (This idea is most effective for decorative items such as bath salts, perfumes, silver hand mirrors, etc.) Or add a chest of drawers for towels and linens, as well as underwear, hosiery, scarves, ties, and T-shirts to make the bathroom double as a dressing room.

Deniece Schofield suggests attaching a shoe bag or wine rack to an empty vertical space and stowing bottles, cans, and tubes in the pockets or cubbyholes; blow-dryers and curling irons also fit neatly into pockets. Or use a recycled toothbrush holder for the blow-dryer—stick it in the hole meant for the cup. Simplest of all, Deniece notes you can tack an empty can to the inside of the vanity or closet door and stash the curling iron

Below: **If you don't want to invest in cabinetry, there's still lots of bathroom storage furniture available in different styles.**

Courtesy Whirlpool

out of sight, yet within reach.

There are also appliance caddies that sit on the counter, as well as grid systems with loops and baskets that attach to the grid for appliances without loops.

Store dirty clothes in a handmade basket or even a plastic wastebasket in the bottom of the bathroom closet or base cabinet. Or simply put a hanging hamper on a hook behind a door. If you have a built-in swing-out clothes hamper, use disposable liners

for easy retrieval of laundry.

If you're remodelling, consider installing a bathroom "wall unit"—a European-style cabinet that covers an entire wall and holds everything from cosmetics to dirty clothes. And plan for the ultimate in bathroom scale storage: a fold-down model recessed into the wall when not in use, like a mini-Murphy bed. You might also think about installing a stackable washer and dryer in the closet, for one-stop laundering.

The ultimate in efficiency is a laundry center in the bathroom. Since water hookups are already there, all you need is a vent for the dryer.

A STEP-BY-STEP GUIDE

PROJECT 6
Above-the-Toilet Storage

To determine the depth of the storage unit, measure the distance from the front of the toilet tank to the wall behind it. This dimension will be the width of a piece of plywood 8 feet long. Cut two of these for the uprights.

Next, measure the width of the tank, adding two inches to give the distance between the two uprights. This will also be the shelf width. Cut a top of ¾" plywood to fit flush over the sides. The back is ¼" plywood flush all around.

Space the shelves to fit your needs. They can be glued and screwed or nailed into place, or you can install track-and-bracket supports for adjustable shelves. Cut three or more shelves of ¾" plywood (or buy shelving to fit). Place the bottom shelf at least 14" above the tank; that way the

top can be removed to service the toilet. Glue and nail or screw all pieces together.

If you want to enclose the space, one option is to use shutters. Department stores, building-supply stores, and hardware stores have assortments of shutters in varying lengths and widths, complete with hinges. (The standard sizes are 6", 7", 8", 9", 10", 11", 12", and 15".) Shop around and select ones that fit as closely as possible the area you want to cover.

Make a frame of 1 x 2 pine to fit flush against the front and top edges of the storage unit. The depth of the frame will depend somewhat on the shutters; it should not extend below the bottom shelf.

For ease of working, build the frame separately on a flat surface, positioning the shut-

ters within and hinging them directly to the frame. Square the frame before attaching the shutters by making both diagonals equal (AB = CD; see illustration); or, use a framing square. Then brace the frame into position with strips of wood nailed temporarily across the corners. These strips remain in place until after the frame has been glued and nailed with finishing nails onto the storage unit.

Fit the shutters so that they close with about a ¹/16" tolerance, or plane them to that gap. Using finishing nails and glue, fasten the frame with shutters already installed to the main unit, making it flush with the top and two sides. Face the bottom of the unit (not covered by frame) with ¾" flat screen mold. Sand and finish to suit your taste.

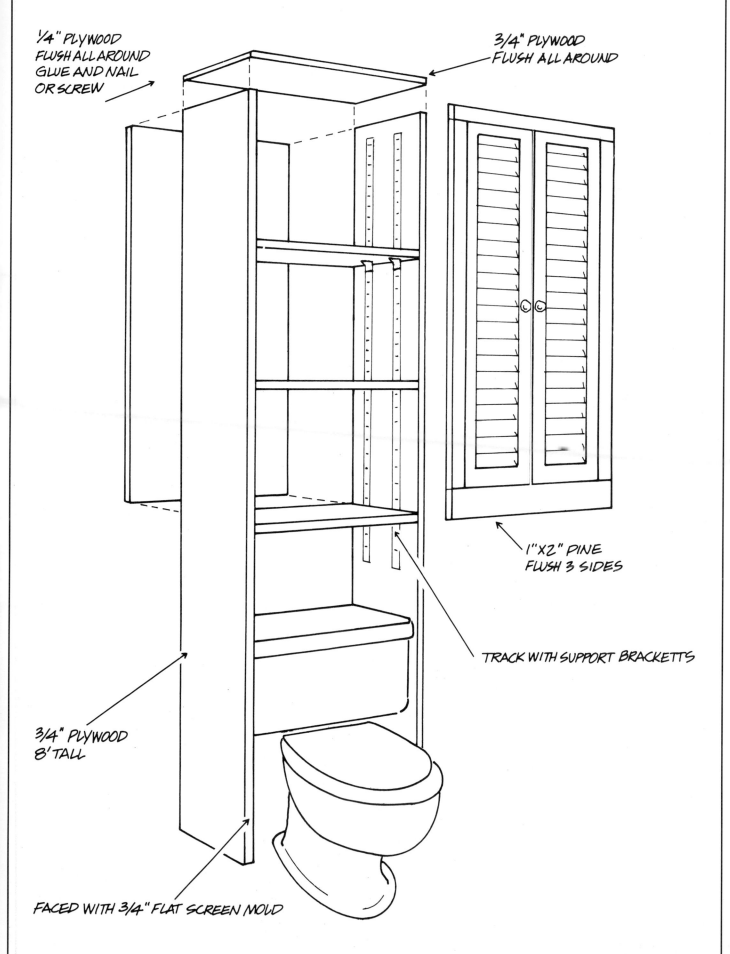

¼" PLYWOOD
FLUSH ALL AROUND
GLUE AND NAIL
OR SCREW

3/4" PLYWOOD
FLUSH ALL AROUND

1"X2" PINE
FLUSH 3 SIDES

TRACK WITH SUPPORT BRACKETTS

3/4" PLYWOOD
8' TALL

FACED WITH 3/4" FLAT SCREEN MOLD

E. Allen McGee/FPG International

Sources and Index

Akro-Mils
Box 989
Akron, OH 44309
Bins, stacking drawers

Amisco Industries Ltd.
Box 250
L'Islet, Quebec
Canada GOR 2CO
Storage furniture

**Armstrong World
    Industries, Inc.**
P.O. Box 3001
Lancaster, PA 17604
Storage furniture

**Arrow Group Industries,
    Inc.**
Pompton Plains, NJ 07444
Shopkeeper cabinet workshop

Beylerian Ltd.
305 East 63rd Street
New York, NY 10021
Furniture, storage systems

Black & Decker
U.S. Household Products
6 Armstrong Road
Shelton, CT 06484
Under-cabinet appliances

California Closet Company
6409 Independence Avenue
Woodland Hills, CA 91367
Closet systems

Closet King
880 Lexington Avenue
New York, NY 10021
Closet systems

Closet Maid
Clairson International
720 South West 17th Street
Ocala, FL 32674
Closet systems

The Creative Organizer
Maxine Ordesky
340 S. Linden Drive
Beverly Hills, CA 90212
**Custom closets and space
planning**

**Culp, Stephanie
The Organization**
5225 Wilshire Boulevard
Suite 415
Los Angeles, CA 90036
(213) 932-8118

Equipto
225 S. Highland Avenue
Aurora, IL 60507
Containers, accessories

Eurodesign Ltd.
12333 Saratoga Sunnyvale
    Road
Saratoga, CA 95070

General Electric Co.
Louisville, KY 40225
Space saving appliances

Heller Designs, Inc.
41 Madison Avenue
New York, NY 10010
Closet grids, record racks

Horizon International
1225 Connecticut Avenue,
    NW
Suite 315
Washington, DC 20036
Storage for TVs, stereos, etc.

**How To Get Organized
    When You Don't Have
    The Time**
    by Stephanie Culp
To Order: Contact
The Organization
5225 Wilshire Boulevard
Suite 415
Los Angeles, CA 90036
(213) 932-8118
or call toll free:
1-800-543-4644

The Idea Center
Deniece Schofield
P.O. Box 492
Bountiful, UT 84010
Organizing products

Ikea Incorporated
Plymouth Commons
Plymouth Meeting, PA 19462
**Storage furniture, organizing
products**

Interlake Inc.
Material Handling Division
550 Warrenville Road
Lisle, IL 60532
Storage bins and systems

**InterMetro Industries
    Corporation**
North Washington Street
Wilkes-Barre, PA 18705
Metal baskets, shelf systems

J Wood
P.O. Box 367
Route 322
Milroy, PA 17063
Cabinets for kitchen and bath

**Knape & Vogt
    Manufacturing Co.**
2700 Oak Industrial Drive, NE
Grand Rapids, MI 61550
Closet hardware

Kartell USA
P.O. Box 1000
Easley, SC 29641
Storage furniture

Lee/Rowan
6333 Etzel Avenue
St. Louis, MO 63133
Closet organizers and accessories

Levelor Lorentzen Inc.
1 Upper Pond Road
Parsippany, NJ 07054

Lockwood
1187 Third Avenue
New York, NY 10021
Wall units and storage furniture

London Closets Ltd.
911 Park Avenue
New York, NY 10021
Custom closet design

Marvin Windows
8043 24th Avenue South
Minneapolis, MN 55420

Molded Fiber Glass Tray Co.
East Erie Street
Linesville, PA 18705
Boxes

Motif Designs
20 Jones Street
New Rochelle, NY 10801

Murphy Door Bed Co., Inc.
5300 New Horizons Boulevard
Amityville, NY 11701
Murphy beds

National Association of Professional Organizers
5350 Wilshire Boulevard
P.O. Box 36E02
Los Angeles, CA 90036
Pro organizers

New Moon
561 Windsor Street
Somerville, MA 02143
Futons and futon furniture

Nutone Inc.
Madison and Red Bank Roads
Cincinnati, OH 45227
Built-in ironing and food processing centers

Organization, USA
1755-C Wilwat Drive
P.O. Box 861
Norcross, GA 30091
Household storage systems

Plain 'n Fancy Kitchens
Route 501
P.O. Box 519
Schaefferstown, PA 17088

Poggenpohl USA Corp.
6 Pearl Court
Allendale, NJ 07401

Quaker Maid
Division of Tappan Corporation
Route 61
Leesport, PA 19533
Kitchen cabinets

Rosalco
P.O. Box 35590
Louisville, KY 40232-5590
Storage furniture

Rubbermaid Incorporated
1147 Akron Road
Wooster, OH 44691
Household organizers

Scandanavian Design, Inc.
117 East 59th Street
New York, NY 10022
Storage furniture

Schulte Corporation
11450 Grooms Road
Cincinnati, OH 45242
Ventilated shelving

Spelman
3001 Veazey Terrace N.W.
Washington, DC 20008

Sturdi-Craft Marketing East
200 Boylston Street
Chestnut Hill, MA 02167
Modular storage systems

SunarHauserman
5711 Grant Avenue
Cleveland, OH 44105
Office systems

Techline
Marshall Erdman & Associates
5117 University Avenue
P.O. Box 5249
Madison, WI 53705
Wall units and storage furniture

Whirlpool
2000 M-63
Benton Harbor, MI 49022

Williams-Sonoma
Hold Everything
Mail Order Department
P.O. Box 7456
San Francisco, CA 94120-7456
Organizing products

Ralph Wilson Plastics Company
McKone & Company, Inc.
1900 Westridge
Irving, TX 75038

Wooden Furniture
508 Canal Street
New York, NY 10013
Custom built Shaker-style storage furniture

Index

METRIC CONVERSION CHART

UNIT	ABBREVIATION OR SYMBOL	METRIC EQUIVALENT
mile	mi	1.609 kilometers
rod	rd	5.029 meters
yard	yd	0.9144 meters
foot	ft *or* '	30.48 centimeters
inch	in *or* "	2.54 centimeters
square mile	sq mi *or* m^2	2.590 square kilometers
acre	acre	4047 square meters
square rod	sq rd *or* rd^2	25.293 square meters
square yard	sq yd *or* yd^2	0.836 square meter
square foot	sq ft *or* ft^2	0.093 square meter
square inch	sq in *or* in^2	6.452 square centimeters
cubic yard	cu yd *or* yd^3	0.765 cubic meter
cubic foot	cu ft *or* ft^3	0.028 cubic meter
cubic inch	cu in *or* in^3	16.387 cubic centimeters
ton	ton	0.907 metric ton
pound	lb or #	0.454 kilogram
ounce	oz	28.350 grams